Games Husbands and Wives Play

Games
Husbands
and
Wives
Play

JOHN W. DRAKEFORD

Broadman Press

Nashville, Tennessee

ISBN: 0–8054–5604–x
4256–04

Dewey Decimal Classification Number: 301.426
Library of Congress Catalog Card Number: 76–132922
Printed in the United States of America

Contents

Games Husbands and Wives Play

Introduction

General Booth's granddaughter sat looking at a cartoon of her famous grandfather. The artist had portrayed the illustrious founder of the Salvation Army as a man in a boat, surrounded by the tempestuous sea of life in which a great number of people battled for survival. The general leaned out over the side of the boat, stretching out his hand to one of the strugglers.

The little girl absorbed in the picture at last commented, "Is Granddaddy trying to shake hands with the man?"

Things are seldom the way they appear.

This is nowhere clearer than in the histrionics that men and women call life.

In one of his most appealing stories Jesus told of children playing in the marketplace. Like youngsters of every age they mimicked their parents as they played.

They loved to play weddings.

Through the busy marketplace they came, a playful rebuke to their parents' serious preoccupation with the stern realities of commerce, food, and raiment.

A piper led the way playing his joyful tune, then came the procession—the bride dressed in mock finery, the groom with assumed solemnity—finally there were the friends singing and applauding.

Not only were they imitating their parents but these Hebrew children were, albeit unconsciously, dramatizing the future experiences of many of their own relationships in the elaborate game of marriage.

Anyone with an eye to see knows that courtship, the preliminary to marriage, is often a highly stylized game in which the two participants make all sorts of maneuvers to entice, tease, avoid commitment, or finally entrap each other.

As complex as all the courting maneuvers may have been, they are only a curtain raiser to a hard fought contest which follows.

It may be in part because marriage is one of the most serious undertakings entered upon by humans, and needs some lighter note to relieve the solemnity, that there are some frivolous moments to offset the tearful mother and solemn clergyman. So comes the obvious tomfoolery.

Much of the horseplay of twentieth-century weddings—tying on cans and shoes or covering the automobile with graffiti—are counterparts of similar activities carried on in ancient times.

The custom of the groom carrying his wife across the threshold of their new home is a carry-over from the Greeks and Romans who expected the groom to engage in a mock fight with the bride's parents, while they, all the time, probably with tongue in cheek, pretended they couldn't bear to part with her. Having wrested her from their parental care, he gathered her up in his arms in triumph and carried her off to their new abode.

All of this is but a prelude and a curtain raiser to some of the games that will go on in the marriage relationship.

GAMESMANSHIP

Games are no longer played just to while away a winter's evening or for the fun of it all. Researchers have discovered the value of educational stimulations and academic games in which the participant plays the role of an individual grappling with a problem that calls for a decision. Educational games come in a variety of forms and include experiences in reacting to propaganda, imaginary speculation on the stock exchange (a very popular subject for games), and participation in the political processes.

The humble parlor game has even taken on a new dimension. Some of these include Sunshine, Ghetto and a Monopoly-type game called Blacks and Whites. They each deal with some aspects of the most serious social problems of race relations and city life.

Some parlor games have moved into the field of interpersonal relations to focus on such questions as personal problems (The Game of Life) or choosing a partner (Dating Game). But, however enjoyable it might be, don't get the idea that you've spent an hour studying psychodynamics or learning the inner secrets of human relationships. While some of the games provide a few limited choices, the crises of life are mostly determined by throwing dice, twisting wheels, or cards haphazardly shuffled and mixed before being drawn without rhyme or reason.

Games like these are not games of skill. As with a plain old poker game, an invisible player who has no interest in the game makes a choice or choices that ultimately determine the outcome. The player's name is chance. In this sense it is gambling and not really gaming.

At the other end of the continuum stands a whole technical

theory of gamesmanship. Closer to this, but still curiously po-
etic, is a book like *Games People Play* which has enjoyed great
popularity. But even to a psychologist with many years of
experience, the whole concept is too complex with its thesis,
dynamisms, social paradigm and psychological paradigm. The
casual reader is likely to get bogged down in psychological
gobbledygook.

Theoretically, when people play games like ticktacktoe or
checkers, chance doesn't enter into the contest and every game
should end in a draw. But a contestant can play these games in
two ways. One way is to "play the board," the other is called
"playing the opponent." In this latter case the contestant not
only plays the game but does it in such a way that he anticipates
how much the game is going to affect his antagonist and gains
control by psychological tactics.

The games contained in this book show how the contestants
can "play the opponent" every inch of the way. The simple
game is presented as a series of choices involving a number of
psychological factors and illustrates some of the ways in which
husbands and wives "play the opponent."

We should learn something from experience, so each game is
followed by "instant replay" presenting a situation in which the
reader can try his hand.

Then having seen a game and attempted to cope with a
similar situation, the reader faces a whole group of ideas that
will help him make a fresh assessment of the situation.

In their involvement in these games some readers may wonder if they have ever participated in such ludicrous maneuvers
in their own lives.

You probably have.

Few "gamers" know what is going on in the marriage game.
The motivations are largely unconscious and many of us go

through complex interactions without the faintest idea as to what is transpiring.

In this collection of games we are trying to discover some of these unconscious motivations and bring them to the level of conscious awareness. Hopefully this discovery will lead us to positive actions.

THE PYRRHIC VICTORY

Beware of the Pyrrhic victory!

The concept of the Pyrrhic victory is fundamental in the series of husband and wife games that we are considering.

When Pyrrhus the King of Epirus led the Grecian forces into southern Italy in the year 281, his 25,000 men, remarkably well equipped with cavalry and elephants, met and defeated the Roman forces.

However his losses were so great that he was compelled to utter his celebrated lament, "Another victory like this and I shall be ruined."

A Pyrrhic victory is costly. Even if you win, you lose.

All the games in this collection lead to Pyrrhic victories.

The primary objective in presenting the game is to help husbands and wives understand just what is happening in some of the strange contests taking place in their marriage.

But insight alone is never enough.

Understanding must give rise to action. With this action concept in mind each game has information and an alternative plan of action to help the participants avoid the Pyrrhic victory.

Format

All the games are set out under a series of headings.

1. *THE NAME OF THE GAME*
2. *THE AIM OF THE GAME*—a brief statement of the objectives.
3. *SPECIAL SKILLS FOR THIS GAME*—an indication of some of the techniques which may help the player.
4. *NUMBER OF PLAYERS*
5. *THE WINNING PLAY*—case study illustrating the course of a game.
6. *INSTANT REPLAY*—a situation which calls for the reader to decide on the best moves.
7. *AVOIDING THE PYRRHIC VICTORY*—a plan of action for making the participant a real winner.

   THE BOX—Many of the games have a box within which is contained factual information on the subject under discussion.

Instructions

You may find these games funny, entertaining, or even a little disturbing.

But if you just sit and laugh or even cry, the effort of both the author and the reader will have been in vain.

This is an action book! Go to it! Take the games one at a time.

* Read the introductory section. Note the name, aim, and special skills for the game. Be prepared for a little irony.
* Carefully follow the winning play—the case study. Project yourself into it.

  Try to relate the case to some experience in your own life or someone you know.
* Now turn to *Instant Replay*.

  Push yourself into the action.

  What do you advise?
* Consult *Avoiding the Pyrrhic Victory*.

  How does your plan compare?

BACKTRACK

THE AIM OF THE GAME: The objective of this little piece of legerdemain is for one player to keep constantly recollecting one incident in his opponent's past and evaluate all present experiences in terms of this long past event.

SPECIAL SKILLS FOR THIS GAME:
* The skillful player of this game must have a vivid memory of the past.
* In any given situation the successful participant must develop the capacity for rapid recall of these past events.
* A competent contestant refuses to listen for any rational reason for the incident but lets his life be completely dominated by an unreal emotional reaction.

NUMBER OF PLAYERS: This game calls for two main contestants but others may be indirectly involved.

THE WINNING PLAY

"Oh what a pretty ring."

Susan smiled blissfully as she received the compliment. There certainly had been rings more elegant and expensive, and diamonds much larger, but common sense had prevailed in their choice. She agreed with Stephen that it was far more important that they have a house to live in than that she impress everybody with a massive stone in her ring.

At first she suspected Stephen was being a little bit chinchy with her. He never hesitated about spending money on himself. He wore the best suits, the most expensive shoes, shirts, and ties, and his cuff links gave the impression that they had obviously cost a packet. But she was glad that he was gradually gaining more sense of the value of money. They had opened a joint account at the bank and the balance continued to build.

No longer needing to impress each other they settled into a more common sense relationship. They seldom ate out now, and when they did it was at one of the more moderately priced eating places.

While Stephen was nowhere near the presidency of his company, he was one of the "up and coming's" in his firm and Susan loved to tell people he was "going somewhere."

Stephen had insisted that she must quit her job the moment they were married, and she had not needed too much pressure. She told the girls at the office that she'd be leaving in June. Not that she really minded working, but she was happy to tell them Stephen insisted.

Just one month before their marriage Stephen had to attend a convention at Las Vegas. Susan didn't much like the idea of him ogling at those show girls, and Stephen, with a twinkle in his eye, joked that it was just one last fling before he settled down to the life of an old married man.

It wasn't really the show girls that excited Stephen. He had watched that joint bank account growing at a snail's pace and he recollected former visits to Vegas and his luck at the tables.

It might well be!

Susan would never forget that night just two weeks before their marriage when Stephen broke the news to her. While in Las Vegas he had gambled away the contents of their joint bank account. He penitently recounted that his motives were right. He had won at first, and it seemed as if he would make a killing which would set them up beautifully and give them a marvelous start in their marriage.

Susan listened incredulously. With a flood of tears she pointed out it wasn't "his" money but "theirs." In fact she had deposited more than he.

That wretched experience overshadowed everything. It descended like a blight on both her work and wedding plans.

She would not now be able to quit work as she had planned. The boss tried to make it easier. He assured her he was glad she wasn't leaving. But she sensed a patronizing attitude of "I told you so," and she recollected his lack of appreciation for Stephen.

The years that followed were difficult. Stephen never quite made it in his job. He changed employment several times. As he told it, someone else was always to blame for his failures.

That horrible night of Stephen's disclosure ever remained before Susan.

Whenever there was trouble at the office, she paused to recall their original plans that she leave work. She envied her friends with their little families and inwardly lamented a motherhood long postponed.

HELP FROM UNEXPECTED SOURCES

One of the unique self-help groups works among convicts. The Seven Steppers have taken Alcoholics Anonymous' Twelve Steps and applied them to a prison situation.

They have come to realize that resentment probably causes more difficulties for the released convict than any other single factor. Following a man's release from prison he may continually remind himself of all the difficulties of and what he considers to be the injustices of prison life.

Entering the outside world with a chip on his shoulder he easily makes a defiant gesture and breaks the law. The result is that he lands back in the penitentiary again.

The fifth step of the Seven Steppers is, "Deciding that our freedom is worth more than our resentments, we are using that power to help us free ourselves from these resentments."

Are we too proud to learn a lesson from a convict?

* * *

A friend of Miss Clara Barton, founder of the American Red Cross, asked her about a particular traumatic event in her life. Miss Barton seemed perplexed.

"Can't you remember?"

Miss Barton replied, "I distinctly remember forgetting it."

In the crisis moments that come in every marriage, one vivid image flashed into Susan's mind as she saw Stephen at the gambling table throwing away the money for which she had worked.

Periodically, there came moments when she could stand it no longer and she verbalized her resentments with a finesse developed by years of practice. She cut Stephen to ribbons with her caustic comments.

Stephen for his part spent more time with the boys or at

work. He had come to anticipate and dread his wife's reactions.

Susan in moments of bitterness lamented a wasted life.

INSTANT REPLAY

Stephen is late in coming home one night. The telephone rings and when Susan answers, Stephen's voice says, "I went out with the boys and I clean forgot to let you know."

Susan immediately recalls the gambling episode and as she sits and waits decides she is going to let him have it when he comes in. She will, of course, remind him of what he did with their savings before marriage.

You call Susan on the phone and in her anger she tells you what has happened and what she plans to do.

How would you advise her?

AVOIDING THE PYRRHIC VICTORY

Remember the Pyrrhic victory? You probably don't. Go back and read page 13.

(1) The resentful person is a reactor rather than an initiator. What other people do determines his attitude toward a given situation. If you want to spend all your life in response to other people, that's OK. Hang on to your resentments. But if you can sense the thrill of taking the initiative in life then do something about settling resentments.

(2) The word resent comes from two Latin words, *sentire,* "to feel" and *re,* "again" or "back." Resentful people are continually looking back—living in the past. If you are to really enjoy life, you must be vividly aware of the reality of the present and the possibilities of the future. Like the apostle Paul you must forget those things which are behind and press towards the mark.

(3) A resentful individual is imprisoned—captured by an emotion. Don't look with disdain upon the addict or the alcoholic. They are at least enslaved by a very tangible drug. You are in bondage to an emotional reaction. Elect to have your freedom.

(4) Remember to forget. The philosopher Kant trusted his servant Lampe for many years. Then he discovered Lampe had systematically robbed him. Although he needed Lampe desperately, he discharged his servant. He sorely missed that helper but wrote in his journal, "Remember to forget Lampe." When an association brings a bygone incident to mind, *remember to forget,* deliberately turn your mind into some other train of thought.

(5) Take a positive action. If the memory of that past event continues to plague you, try to focus on the part, small though it may be, that you played in it. If you took a wrong action, at the time or since, undertake some plan of restitution and put it right. An offended conscience can often help to keep the past alive.

(6) Be an initiator. Keep the situation under control. When the memory of that past event floats on to the screen of your mind, make a counter move. Recall some of the experiences you enjoy or an idea that gives you fresh confidence.

"Nothing on earth consumes a man like resentment."

Nietzche

GAME 2

HURT

WHY DOSEN'T SHE JUST CLOBBER ME AND GET IT OVER WITH...

THE AIM OF THE GAME: In this contest the key to a contestant's success is his capacity to keep the initiative by maintaining a pose of being "hurt."

SPECIAL SKILLS FOR THIS GAME:
* The player convinces himself that he is specially sensitive, "like a finely strung violin."
* A hair-trigger response by which a minor irritation revives a past event.
* A competent contestant must remember the two different types of silence:
  Creative Silence—indicating a keen interest by giving another person your undivided attention. Don't use this!
  Belligerent silence—It says, "I'm just going to cut myself off and refuse to listen to you." This is it! Master this technique and you will have a devastating weapon.

NUMBER OF PLAYERS: Two main contestants but other players in contact with the two main protagonists help to condition them and the way they play the game.

THE WINNING PLAY

However on earth did Jim and Mary Schweitzer get together?

They're so completely different.

Jim is the tall taciturn type—man of few words. He pines for solitude. If you were to ask him his idea of paradise, he would tell you: a lonely island somewhere, a quiet mountain cave some place where never an intruder or a telephone bell called for attention.

Mary is quite the opposite. She loves people—lots of people. Her ideal position would be greeter at a convention. She loves to grasp their hands, smile into their faces, inquire about their health, engage in the give and take of lively conversation.

She is a sort of feminine Hubert Humphrey.

Jim and Mary might well be the classic example of Winch's theory of complimentary needs. He says people frequently choose their opposites for mates because they compliment each other.

After an exciting courtship during which Jim delighted to listen to Mary's excited babblings and she in turn responded to his attention, they married and set up their little home.

In rapid succession Mary gave birth to three children and was soon settled into the life of a fairly typical American mother.

As she faced the usual hazards of family life; measles, chicken pox, PTA, the budget, she sometimes thought about her premarriage days when she was in a constant swirl of social events and spent her waking moments meeting people.

Jim, on the other hand, has moved into a new position with the department store for which he works. Because of his quiet attitude they send him to work in customer relations.

All Jim's days are spent in listening to an unending series of complaints about the store, its products and its service. By the time the day is over, Jim begins to dream about home.

He feels thankful that a man's home is his castle. He pictures himself as arriving home, sinking into an easy chair, burying himself in that new book, and forgetting all about customer relations and complaining people.

Mary too is anticipating the evening. After a day with those three small children, she has the mounting feeling that the children are closing in on her. All of life must be seen through childish eyes. In her despair she wonders about those bygone social relationships.

Thank goodness Jim will be home later. That will be her moment.

Mary has been reading the *Ladies Home Journal* and was greatly taken with an article "Communication in Marriage." The writer had pointed out the importance of communication and suggested one of the problems was that most husband-wife conversations had no objective, no purpose—they just petered out.

In her mind Mary determined Jim and she needed communication and was determined to prepare carefully for it. Mentally, she laid out an agenda of the evening tête-a-tête.

They really should decide about John, their eldest boy, who has been rather sassy of recent days. Perhaps Jim should have a man to man talk with him.

Then there was this Middle East crisis. She was so confused, but all she heard were the newscasts. Jim was out in the big wide world, and he would be able to help her.

And they really should finish up with something to stretch their intellectual muscles. She heard the preacher speaking about existentialism a few Sundays ago and she didn't really know what he meant. When they are involved in their dialogue, she will ask Jim to explain it to her.

Completely carried away with her idea, Mary made sure she had everything moving on schedule, changed into one of her prettier dresses and prepared for Jim's arrival.

Jim's entrance was hardly the event of the year.

He came in through the back door, buzzed the children, pecked Mary, dropped into his favorite chair and buried his head in a book as if he were in fact on that lonely island about which he had so often dreamed.

To say Mary was frustrated is to put it mildly. After all her planning, all this preparation was apparently in vain.

The article in the *Ladies Home Journal* hadn't anticipated such a situation as this. Well she wasn't going to take it lying down.

"Jim."

"Yes."

"Did you have a good day?"

"Mm."

Not too promising. Perhaps she was not specific enough.

"You know that customer with whom you were having so much trouble?"

"Yes."

"Did he come back?"

"Yes."

"What happened?"

"Fixed him up."

In these two minds two opposite processes are taking place.

Jim is thinking, "Doesn't she realize that I've been working hard all day with people driving me mad with stupid complaints. Surely I'm entitled to some peace when I get home."

Mary's mind ran down another track, she could not help but think of the crass injustice of her situation. "Can't he understand that I've been at home with three children all day with no one to talk to and I desperately need some conversation. I'm not going to put up with it any longer."

So Mary decides to throw out a challenge, "John are you going to talk to me or aren't you?"

Whereupon Jim responds with vehemence, "Mary, will you shut up?"

The moment Jim exploded he knew it was wrong, and he would have given anything to get those words back.

But he'll not get them back. They have suddenly been immortalized. He'll be reminded of them intermittently in the years ahead.

Jim is now ready to talk. He'll discuss the children, world affairs, anything—but not Mary.

In those strange games which husbands and wives play it is very important to keep the initiative. It is as significant to the marriage game as the service is in a game of tennis.

Once you've gained the initiative it is important to keep it. It would be disastrous to let your spouse take over.

So Mary keeps Jim on the run.

And she does it with the most curious technique of all—silence.

It doesn't matter what Jim says; he cannot evoke any response from Mary. With the silent treatment she cuts him down to size.

By her determined attitude Mary, like some medieval torturer, gradually wears him down.

MARKS OF RELATIONSHIP

1. A healthy relationship grows from communication by sharing and listening to another person.
2. A good relationship is facilitated when two people are aware of each other's faults and strengths and yet each appreciates the other.
3. In a mature relationship two people can have entirely different points of view and one can reject the other's argument without rejecting him as a person.
4. A wholesome relationship allows two people to be themselves and maintain a closeness without the need to manipulate each other.
5. In a sound relationship each person seeks to help the other by specific actions.

Tuesday night, Wednesday morning, Wednesday night.

No matter what Jim says she responds with monosyllables.

The whole affair drags on for another ten days before they finally get back on to an even keel again.

INSTANT REPLAY

Just two days after Jim and Mary's encounter, Jim was driving home from work. The burden of his fractured relationship with his wife lay heavy upon him.

As he drove past the church he saw the preacher's car parked outside and wheeled around into the parking area, left the car, and headed for the minister's study.

Sitting opposite his minister he somewhat shamefacedly related the whole story.

The pastor sat and listened. He knew Jim just needed to get it all off his chest.

When Jim had finished his story, he looked up and said, "Well preacher what should I do?"

What would you tell him?

AVOIDING THE PYRRHIC VICTORY

1. Become aware of the infantile nature of this behavior. If the children took this attitude we would call it sulking. Naming it righteous indignation does not excuse it.

2. A wife should try to understand the problems her husband faces. Learn as much as you can about his work and be aware of the trouble spots he is likely to run into. It will help you if you can anticipate some of these.

3. Husbands too. Because you are away from home for such a good proportion of any one day you may find it difficult to appreciate the peculiar problems of a housewife. Recollect the time when in an emergency you looked after some of the household chores. Remember those frustrations?

4. There are no perfect people. Everybody makes mistakes. Realize you belong to the club. When you make a mistake, admit it. The quicker you are to acknowledge your mistake the sooner you will restore a relationship.

5. If your spouse makes a mistake, don't demand your pound of flesh. Be prepared to give him the benefit of the doubt.

6. *Attack the act, not the person.* When your spouse does something of which you disapprove, be careful how you respond. Help your partner realize that you still love him but the action bothers you. Not, "It's just like you to do a silly thing like that," but rather, "I love you and appreciate all the good things you do but you weren't at your best when you did this."

"Make the most of your lonely bath in self pity, it will certainly mess up your marriage relationship."

GAME 3

DON'T SAY
"I TOLD YOU SO..."

I KNOW, I KNOW

THE AIM OF THE GAME: To bluff your opponent by refusing to listen to her suggestions.

SPECIAL SKILLS FOR THIS GAME:
* A capacity to give the impression of expertize in a particular field.
* A knack for pouring scorn on any suggestions offered by your spouse no matter how valid they might be.
* A fierce optimism that everything will turn out all right.

NUMBER OF PLAYERS: In its widest application any number can play but there must be one person in a decision-making position. In this version there are two main contestants, a husband and a wife. Children may play subsidiary roles.

THE WINNING PLAY

"Don't you think we should have been there by now?"
Louise *knew* they should have reached their destination by

this time, but she was asking a question in the hope of helping David realize they were in unknown territory and lost.

It had been a very enjoyable trip, long in the planning. Getting the maps from AAA, making out the budget, planning and revising the route.

The children provided their quota of problems as they blew hot and cold. At first all enthusiastic about the trip, as the time drew near their interest waned and they became aware of all the advantages of staying home for the summer.

Louise worried over the children but David simply put his foot down and insisted they come. She could see the children's point of view, and tried to be the mediator. However, in her most impartial moments, she realized the children really should go along.

The trip from Miami to Georgia had proved interesting, but after the first few hours the children were bored and began to complain. As the day progressed, David became less communicative as he gazed ahead, lips tight and a determined look on his face.

He wasn't familiar with the route but had marked out the map and given it to Louise. Periodically, he called on her to check their position.

Poor Louise. She was an excellent housekeeper, a superlative mother, and the world's worst map reader.

She never could quite get the hang of all the symbols, the distinction of dotted lines, solid red or blue, nor work out which was south or east or what the little numbers represented.

It irritated her when David would suddenly thrust the map at her and call on her to read it and let him know their location.

She often fretted within herself. It was all right for him. He could spend hours poring over maps, plotting routes, marking

MATURITY

The word mature simply means to grow, and the maturing person must be aware that life is a continual process of growth and development.

A maturing person will have a number of characteristics.

* The maturing person is a creature of emotions but not their slave. Emotional reactions are essential for survival but they are primitive responses. We must beware of reacting at an earlier emotional level and grow emotionally as well as physically and intellectually.

* The maturing person is guided by long-term purposes rather than immediate desires. A popular definition of maturity is "the capacity to postpone pleasure," and it contains a great deal of truth. Allport says it in another way, "Every mature personality may be said to travel towards a port of destination, selected in advance, on to several ports in succession."

* The maturing person has a perspective on life beyond his own self-interest. All of life is a socializing process during which we learn the futility of self-centeredness. A person with no sense of involvement with other people will always remain immature.

* The maturing person develops a capacity for self-objectivication. Socrates asserted, "I must first know myself," and unfortunately self-knowledge doesn't come easily. We must cultivate the ability to periodically take an inventory of our strengths and weaknesses.

* The maturing person has a unifying philosophy of life. The really mature person has some focal point around which the processes of the personality are gathered. Obviously our individual faith in Christ is of primary importance here.

out distances, determining the sizes of cities. But she had been hard at work about household tasks.

They had made a reservation in a motel in Wilmington for that evening and after the earlier delays the night began to overtake them.

With the growing realization that he had misjudged the distance David's patience continued to wear thin.

Periodically, he pulled over to the side of the road, seized hold of the map, and struggled to work out their location.

Louise had learned from long experience that when David was in this sort of situation the least said the better. But as he pulled up opposite Bill's Truck Stop, Louise could restrain herself no longer, "David, why don't we ask someone?"

"Ask someone?" Her spouse looked at her as if she had lost every vestige of her sanity.

David poured out his scorn on the suggestion. What was the matter with her? Did he not have a perfectly good map? Why did he need to be asking some local yokel?

Louise subsided into silence.

David pulled out into the highway following the route he knew would get him to his destination.

Thirty minutes later saw them once again on the side of the road with David determinedly gazing at the map.

Louise made another try, "Honey, don't you think it would be a good idea to ask somebody?"

David heaved a sigh. The crass ignorance and stubborness of women. He reminded Louise of the time they had been in England and while visiting Windsor they asked one of the locals the way to Eton. The man had stood there with a vacant look on his face. Although Eton was only a quarter of a mile away, the poor dolt couldn't tell them how to get there.

Once again they got underway. The shadows of night deepened. David remarked that it was just as well they had paid a deposit on their room. The motel would have to keep it for them.

Louise inwardly commented that by the same token if they didn't find the motel they'd lost their deposit.

Somehow or another Louise managed to keep her silence, but fumed within herself, "Goodness only knows where we are, why doesn't David ask somebody? Oh the obstinancy of men."

As they drove on, David clenched his teeth. He had the dawning awareness that he was lost—hopelessly lost—lost as much as if he were in the middle of the Sahara Desert or back of Timbuktu.

David realized the time had come to swallow his pride.

He wheeled into the service station and as the attendant approached him asked, "How much further is it to Wilmington?"

"Wilmington?" The attendant looked bewildered and hurried off to consult the boss.

"Just like I said, these men don't know their own backyards," commented David with masculine satisfaction.

The boss approached, "You want to get to Wilmington?"

"Yes."

"I'm afraid you've overshot it by about fifty miles.

"I'll tell you what you do. Go back down this highway. Measure it on your speedo. About forty-nine miles. Watch out for a big truck stop on the right hand side of the highway. It's called Bill's Truck Stop. You can't miss it. Turn right there and the town is about three miles down the highway."

Louise bit her tongue to keep from saying, "Why didn't you ask when I told you."

They turned around and headed back down the highway towards Bill's Truck Stop.

INSTANT REPLAY

David and Louise have dreamed about a cabin at the lake. A friend told them about one on Spirit Lagoon. Sunday afternoon they met the realtor out at the site and he showed it to them.

On that beautiful sunny afternoon it looked attractive, and David grew more enthusiastic by the minute. But Louise could not help but notice how old it looked and the bad arrangement of the closets. She wondered about termites.

The real estate man hinted he had another party also interested, but if they would sign the contract it could be theirs.

Louise knew David had virtually no knowledge about building. She noted his interest and the way he said, "Well honey, I think we ought to buy it, don't you?"

She knew he wasn't asking for an opinion just a confirmation, but she had serious doubts.

What should Louise do?

AVOIDING THE PYRRHIC VICTORY

1. While we all need a sense of our own importance let us be realistic and face the fact that we made mistakes. And we are in good company. Gladstone said, "No man ever became great or good except through many and great mistakes."

2. Although it may hurt us to acknowledge our failures it has the reverse effect on others. A man who admits his failure disarms his accuser.

3. The ability to confess a fault is indicative of inner strength. One adage says, "A man is never stronger than when he is admitting his weaknesses."

4. Don't procrastinate about owning up to your "goof." In their twelve steps Alcoholics Anonymous suggests, "Continued to make personal inventory and when we were wrong promptly admitted it." The sooner you acknowledge your error the easier it will be.

5. Remember that two heads are better than one. Your spouse knows much more than you give credit for and may bring some significant insights to the relationship.

6. Part of the maturing process is learning to take an objective view of ourselves. Gordon Allport says that one of the indications of maturity is the ability to laugh at oneself. Learn to laugh at your own foibles.

"Only the ignorant know everything."

GAME
4

DIVIDE TO CONQUER

THE AIM OF THE GAME: To keep uncooperative parents off balance by dealing with them separately.

SPECIAL SKILLS FOR THIS GAME:
* A capacity to capitalize on childish innocence presented in such a way that parents would never suspect any ulterior motivations.
* An awareness that parents fall for gestures of love and affection which quickly break down their hostilities and antagonisms.
* An ability to find some issue on which parents have a variation in opinion and then exploit the issue.

NUMBER OF PLAYERS: At least three which must include two parents and one child. The number can be expanded with exciting possibilities as the number of child participants is increased.

THE WINNING PLAY

"You just wait until your father gets home. He'll give you the paddling of your life."

The moment she said it, Charlotte Simpson realized it wasn't the best strategy, but she was absolutely fed up with Sheila.

That eleven-year-old could create more difficulties than any two children. Because she had a heavy schedule, Charlotte warned Sheila to be home on the dot of 4:00 P.M. Sheila forgot the admonition and after school had gone home with her friend Joan.

Charlotte had to depend on Sheila to look after the two-year-old while she rushed down to the store to straighten up their account. By the time Sheila came in at 5:30, she was thoroughly irked and let fly with a stream of recriminations.

Sheila could not understand why her mother should be upset just because she had gone to Joan Johnson's home. Surely Mother ought to understand that a growing girl must have some social life.

As soon as Mother mentioned Daddy's name, the situation became serious. Mr. Billy Simpson was a no-nonsense father, and once his wife got him really stirred up he dispensed discipline with a heavy hand.

So it happened that as Mr. Billy Simpson came driving up within three blocks of his home who should flag him down but his daughter, Sheila.

Seldom had she been so friendly as she told him about schoolwork and church and finally let him know that very few friends of hers were as fortunate as she. It was so good to have a father with whom she could talk.

Sheila snuggled up to her daddy, "All the girls say that I've got such a wonderful daddy that I'm the luckiest girl."

Small wonder that when Charlotte tried to tell her spouse about Sheila's earlier irresponsible behavior, she found him only half listening and pointing out that you can't put an old head on young shoulders. Surely she remembered that when she was a girl she didn't have a good sense of time.

● ● ● ● ● ● ● ● ● ● ● ● ● ● ● ● ● ● ● ●

Two nights later came an encounter with Billy, Jr.

Billy was about normal for a healthy sixteen-year-old, fair in his academic record, a pretty good basketball player, an enthusiastic but somewhat indifferent strummer of the guitar. But whatever he lacked in the educational, sports, or music fields, he made up for with unbounded confidence.

He had reached the stage in life when his mind was preoccupied with automobiles. By taking a driver's education course at school he had gained his license and spent a good proportion of his waking moments devising ways of getting behind the wheel of the family car.

Planning his strategy carefully he offered to help with the dishes that evening, and that move itself ought to have been sufficient warning to Mrs. Simpson. Dishes finished, Billy casually mentioned that he needed a special book from the downtown library and asked his mother, "Do you think it will be OK for me to drive down to the library?"

Mrs. Simpson had certain questions in her mind about Billy's driving prowess, but he had been so helpful that she hated to turn him down flat, "Why don't you ask your father?"

In her mind she half planned to get a signal to her husband but the phone rang and long-winded Mrs. Sensor from the PTA launched into a long account of the plans for the annual carnival.

THE POSITIVE REFUSAL

The actress in the musical, "Oklahoma" lamented, "I'm just a little girl who couldn't say no," but everyone must learn to use this two letter word. It will never be easy but there are some ways of taking the pain out of the process.

* Remove the refusal from the personal basis. Make it clear that while you appreciate the other person and his request, because of the premises under which you are operating, you must refuse.

* Indicate that you don't enjoy saying, "no." Work the conversation around to a moment when you say, "Nothing would please me more than to go along with you, and I hate to do it, but I must say no.

* Give evidence that you have studied the situation. Don't convey the impression that this is an arbitrary ill-considered decision. Comment on factors involved in denying the request.

* Help him say no to himself. Show him the factors involved in such a way that he may reach the negative conclusion before you break the news to him.

* Suggest some factors which might have changed the no to yes. Explain some of the considerations and proceed, "Now if the situation had been . . ." "If your request had . . . ," "But you realize. . ."

* Help him see the situation from your perspective. Try to show him how it looks from a viewpoint other than his, "If you were in my place, what would you do?"

* Let your no be said in the nicest way. Speaking of the president of a great institution one of his employees said, "He sometimes refused my requests, but he did it so kindly and graciously that I never felt upset by his refusal." This is the way to do it.

Billy disappeared into the den.

Mr. Simpson hardly looked up. Buried in his book he had no burning desire to visit with his offspring.

Billy Jr. took the initiative, "I have to go down to the library, Dad. I've talked to Mother about it, and she says if it's all right with you I can take the car."

"Take the car." Billy Simpson had always had misgivings about his son and heir's driving ability. Well, apparently Charlotte was satisfied, so he reached into his pocket and handed over the keys.

An hour later the phone rang.

Charlotte answered and heard Junior's distressed voice. He'd had a wreck over on the north side of the city miles away from the library.

When she broke the news to her husband, Mr. Simpson blew his top and demanded to know why she had agreed to let Billy take the car.

It is better to draw a veil over the next ten minutes as George and Charlotte blamed each other for the problem situation with the car.

INSTANT REPLAY

Mr. Simpson's secretary announced, "Your cute little daughter, Sheila, is on the phone."

When Mr. Simpson answered, Sheila told him the good news that she has made four A's. "Just wait till you see my report card, you're going to be proud of me."

"I'm always proud of you, Honey. I can see now that our family is probably going to produce the first woman astronaut."

Mr. Simpson knew it was of the utmost importance that he give his daughter the praise that would encourage her.

"Daddy."

"Yes, Honey."

"Do you think it would be all right for me to go to a slumber party at Marylyn Graham's tonight? Mrs. Graham has to know right away and I've already tried to contact Mother but I think she is at the beauty parlor. Please, Daddy."

What should Mr. Simpson do?

AVOIDING THE PYRRHIC VICTORY

1. Make sure you understand the children's proposition. Get all the information. They are probably telling the truth, but even the truth looks different when you know the whole story.

2. Don't talk to each other through the children. You can discuss it in their presence, spelling out the pros and cons, or you can insist on the right to talk together and then announce your decision and perhaps the reasons for it. But make sure you have a face-to-face conversation with your spouse.

3. Don't be stampeded into a hasty decision—take your time —things are seldom as urgent as children make them out to be.

4. If discipline is to be administered, it should be done immediately. Don't hold judgment over the heads of the children by threatening, "Wait until your father comes home." There is a good chance he won't like being used as a policeman.

5. Keep a united front. Even if your spouse is making a mistake and you feel tempted to correct her, don't do it. Don't interfere. Perhaps afterward you can discuss the wisdom of the action but don't do it in front of the children.

"While Julius Caesar may have devised the strategy of dividing to conquer, children have perfected the technique in their relationships with their parents."

GAME
5

IF I SAY ANYTHING TO HIM IT WILL GO TO HIS HEAD...

DON'T TELL

THE AIM OF THE GAME: To praise your mate behind her back but never to her face.

SPECIAL SKILLS FOR THIS GAME:
* Learn to keep a poker face whenever your partner tells you of a special feat or accomplishment.
* Realize that praise may spoil people and compliments give them a swollen head.
* Give yourself a sense of satisfaction by bragging about your partner to other people who will all say what a wonderful husband you must be.

NUMBER OF PLAYERS: Any number can play. In some rounds it is just two players and in other places it requires a number of participants but the individual skill of just one person is important.

THE WINNING PLAY

Fran Parkington, mother of four, graduate of State Teachers' College, plays bridge, water skis, serves her family delicious meals, and loves PTA.

She came up the hard way, and during her years of teacher training she resolved she would involve the people in the community in the work of the school no matter what.

In her first teaching assignment she not only tried to drum the three R's into the children's heads but she gave equal attention to their parents. Looking back on it in later years, people in the community often recalled when Fran taught their children.

In that year the school mimeograph machine ran hot, as Fran poured out a constant stream of notes, supplemented and reinforced by phone calls that invited the parents to conferences about their children, but above everything else promoted PTA as it had never been promoted before.

In her enthusiasm she presented an invitation to PTA as if it were a summons to meet the President of the United States. Fran had a special skill in motivating the children to plead with their fathers and mothers to make sure their room had the best attendance at the monthly meeting.

Many a father, pestered by persistent children, fervently wished someone would call off this eager beaver teacher.

And Harold Parkington was the man who unwittingly answered their prayers.

Harold literally swept Fran off her feet.

That insistent young insurance executive had such a winning way with her that she could not say nay to his wooing.

Even as she let her heart take over, Fran still convinced

herself that modern couples planned their pregnancies and she would still continue on with her teaching. And Harold agreed.

But she discovered that only the unmarried and the uninitiated have complete confidence in contraception. Three months after the wedding ceremony, she became pregnant and that brought her teaching career to a conclusion.

In rapid succession came three more children. Fran settled down to enjoy them and presided gracefully over her little household.

Harold, for his part, felt he could leave the affairs of the domestic front in Fran's capable hands and immersed himself in his business.

When she had enrolled two of the children in school, Fran felt the time had come for her to do her bit for that institution. Naturally her mind turned to PTA.

She joined the PTA. Not reluctantly, but willingly and gladly, and from the first day of attendance happily accepted any responsibility when requested.

Harold grumbled a little when the evening meetings came and Fran insisted he should come with her. However, inwardly, he felt not a little proud as members of the group told him how much they all valued Fran. But, PTA was not really his cup of tea. While he enjoyed meeting some of the people, he soon became bored with the meetings and somewhat restive and anxious to get on his way.

On the evening of the PTA annual meeting Harold was involved in an important dinner engagement with a client. The client brought his wife along with him and as Harold explained that Fran would have been with them but for the PTA meeting, he was painfully aware of the look of disappointment that fluttered across the face of his client's wife.

THE NEEDS OF MAN

Psychologist Maslow says, "Man is a perpetually wanting animal." Every individual has certain needs which when first encountered seem the most important single thing in life.

However when these needs have been satisfied, new needs emerge. So man is a perpetually wanting animal

Physiological needs are basic to survival but once food and drink has been supplied the individual wants to live in an orderly world and his safety needs become obvious. Assured of safety his love needs demand attention and when provided for are replaced by his esteem needs.

At the top of this hierarchy Maslow places self-actualization. What the individual can become, he must become.

A realization of the needs for esteem and self-actualization emphasizes how important it is for us to give recognition and consideration to our spouse. It will never be enough for us to claim we have provided economic security and that is sufficient. We must always be aware of needs for esteem and self-actualization.

Perhaps the woman felt slighted by the absence of Fran. She was very difficult in the discussion which followed. She raised all sorts of problems about the contract and made so many minor points that her husband finally felt obliged to remonstrate with her.

That certainly didn't help.

The woman lapsed into an obstinate silence, and the evening finally concluded with no contract signed and Harold thoroughly frustrated.

Fran waited eagerly at home for Harold's return. As he came in the door, she hurried over and gave him a hug and said, "Honey, you're going to be so proud of me."

"Oh."

"Yes, your wife was elected president of the PTA tonight."

Harold knew what the situation called for. He should have let out a whoop of joy, swept her off her feet, and congratulated her. But after that supper experience he not only couldn't raise a whoop, but would have found it difficult to whisper.

He lamely commented, "Congratulations, that's fine."

As Fran watched him disappear into his study a feeling of utter frustration swept over her.

The moment she'd looked forward to for so long, and now Harold refused to share it with her.

The following morning the men stood around drinking coffee in the staff room.

Harold was speaking, "Last night Fran was elected president of the PTA. Am I proud? I tell you I couldn't feel better if she had become the President of the United States."

On and on he went. Some of the men began to look a trifle bored.

Sydney Solomon, who had the reputation for being a particularly poor husband and spent a good deal of his time evading his marriage responsibilities said, "Well, Harold you must be the ideal husband. You have the sort of attitude that women really go for."

INSTANT REPLAY

In the midst of a rush to get the small children bathed and the supper prepared the phone begins to ring.

Fran tells her oldest girl to answer it and tell whoever it is to call back later.

June comes to the bathroom door, "It's Daddy, and he says he must talk with you."

Fran heaves a sigh, wipes her hands, and picks up the phone, "Yes, Harold!"

"Honey, I got wonderful news. I've just been made treasurer of the company."

What should Fran say?

AVOIDING THE PYRRHIC VICTORY

1. Accentuate the positive. Emerson said, "Every man I meet is in some way my superior." Forget your spouse's weaknesses; concentrate on the strong points.

2. After years of study, William James concluded, "The deepest principle in human nature is the craving to be appreciated." Remember this in your relations with your helpmeet.

3. Build your partner's affection for you by a positive action. Dale Carnegie says the fundamental principle for making people like you is, "Always make the other person feel important."

4. Give at least as much praise before your partner's face as you do behind his back.

5. If you *must* criticize (and *must* you?):

Find something to commend before offering any suggestions.

Discuss your own mistakes before criticizing your spouse.

6. In marriage there are certain things that concern a husband and wife alone. Correcting faults is one of them. Never, never correct your spouse in the presence of others.

"You may be liberal in your praise where praise is due; it costs nothing, it encourages much."

Horace Mann

GAME
6

GET OUT OF MY WAY, CAT...

PECK ORDER

THE AIM OF THE GAME: To select a person who cannot strike back as a subject upon whom to vent hostility.

SPECIAL SKILLS FOR THIS GAME:
* A capacity to react quickly and unthinkingly.
* An awareness of the "pecking order"—there are some people whom you cannot attack—your boss for example, but if you've got the right type of wife and submissive employees, they're just right. Children also make excellent targets.
* An inflated sense of your self importance so that you never see your own faults.

NUMBER OF PLAYERS: Not more than ten players can participate, preferably a smaller number. When too many play the effect is sometimes lost as the game proceeds.

AN EXAMPLE OF A GAME OF PECK ORDER

J. B., President of Unwin, Inc., is trying desperately to be his tactful best. He stands before his employees to remind them that at Unwins they are all one big happy family. He reminds them of the new hospitalization policy which is typical of the company's concern for each member of its staff.

He pauses, "However there is one little matter I want to mention. Lunch is from 12:00 to 12:45. It has come to my attention that some of you are slipping out early and staying away later. Please don't do this. Twelve to twelve forty-five."

Within himself J. B. decides that he is going to set the example so he waits that day until the tick of twelve before heading out to meet a crony for lunch.

When he arrives at the restaurant his friend is not there. He waits for him. And when at last he arrives they take their place at the table and fret out the inordinately long time it takes to get service.

One o'clock, one-fifteen, one-thirty!

J. B. breaks loose and jumps into his car to head out for town.

He's making wonderful time. So good in fact that he sees a flashing light in his rear vision mirror.

He pulls over to the side of the road, and the police officer proceeds to give him a safety lecture followed by a traffic ticket.

As J. B. moves off, he keeps carefully within the speed limit but his mind is racing, "They wouldn't be out catching the criminals . . . nor putting down riots . . . not catching teenage hot-rodders . . . just catching an innocent citizen trying to get back to work on time."

When at last J. B. gets back to the office, he is in a filthy mood.

Shortly after J. B.'s return the sales manager walks in.

"Hi, J. B."

"Hi."

"J. B. you know that sales deal I was supposed to put through this morning . . ."

"Yes."

"I . . . flubbed it."

"You flubbed it?"

It wasn't so much what J. B. said as the way he said it.

After a difficult session, the salesman left J. B.'s office and headed out for his own sanctum.

He couldn't settle down to his work. As his eyes roamed the desk, he had a vague feeling of something left undone. He pressed the buzzer.

As his secretary came hurrying in she smiled, "You buzzed."

"Yes, Mrs. Brown. Those letters we were writing for the eleven-thirty mail. Did we get them away?"

"Oh, those letters. You'll never guess."

"Oh?"

"I forgot all about them."

"You forgot . . ."

The sales manager proceeds to tell her what happens through careless work. He sort of implies that because those letters didn't get away the whole company might easily go into bankruptcy.

It's the secretary's turn now. She withdraws from the office and heads out for her little nook.

As she leaves his office she passes by the receptionist's desk.

PECK ORDER

When you call a human being a "chicken" the comparison may not be as demeaning as we popularly imagine. Some social scientists have found that chickens and humans have some things in common.

One investigator discovered that chickens have a peck order. He found that in a flock of chickens, one hen generally dominated all the rest. She could peck all of the other hens who did not dare peck in return.

Another hen pecked all except the top hen. The rest of the flock arranged themselves in a descending order which ended in an unfortunate hen who was pecked by all but could not peck anyone else.

This fascinating investigation has given rise to the idea of the "peck order."

From our perspective there is one remarkable difference in the peck order of humans and hens. The cocks do not peck the hens, so that in any flock two peck orders—one for males, the other for females.

Perhaps the moral is that husbands and wives should not peck each other!!!

The receptionist is a cheery little soul who feels the weight of all the office morale is upon her shoulders and she decides to try and help the secretary.

"The boss sure was chewing you out in there."

Mrs. Brown responds in a moment and tells the receptionist what she thinks about people who go around poking their nose into other people's business.

And as it becomes obvious to her—the secretary—that she —the receptionist—doesn't have enough to do. She will remedy that little matter.

She hurries off to her desk and returns with a basket of work which she dumps down alongside the receptionist.

The receptionist falls into a disillusioned and dispirited frame of mind, That's the way it goes. You just try to help somebody, and they turn on you.

At this unfortunate moment a hapless salesman comes in through the office door.

He's been reading *How to Win Friends and Influence People,* and in his mind he is rehearsing his warm up procedure. "Head erect, shoulders square, smile on my face, I am going to get my quota early this week. I can do it."

As he approaches the receptionist, he notices she is kind of hunched up.

He reaches over and touches her arm with a remarkable result.

She comes uncoiled, "Keep your cotton picking hands off me. I can't stand men who go around mauling women . . ."

The amazed salesman stands and listens to the denunciation, then, deciding there is no possibility of a sales here, retreats.

Once outside the door he puzzles over his experience, however on earth did that happen?

The more he thinks of it the more depressed he becomes. "I can't sell when I feel like this. I'm just going to give up and go home."

His wife has been hard at work cleaning out the house, and as her husband enters the back door she turns to greet him.

"Why, Honey. What are you doing home so early today? I thought you were going to win friends and influence people and get your quota early this week."

He responds by telling her he'll get his quota when he wants to get his quota. Has he ever failed to bring home the salary check?

DISPLACED HOSTILITY

Hostility may be said to be displaced when it is engendered by one situation and projected on to another.

In the case presented here the hostility went from J. B. to his salesmanager, the salesmanager to his secretary, the secretary to the receptionist, the receptionist to the salesman, the salesman to his wife, his wife to the small boy, the small boy to the cat.

How much simpler it would have been if J. B. could have only kicked that cat!

And why does this house look as if a tornado has just been through it? What has she been doing all day?

He stamps on through the house to leave his wife hurt and angry.

Utterly frustrated, Marjory turns around to see Junior, age 6, about to twist the "on-off" control on the TV set.

That did it! She'd had enough. Already he'd had more than his quota before the video tube.

She rushed over and paddled him good and hard and pushed him out into the backyard.

And Junior, disgusted with life, ran and kicked the cat!

INSTANT REPLAY

Let us rerun the case.

The salesman undoubtedly pulled a boo-boo. He went home and took it all out on his little wife. It was unfair to her.

However in all honesty we have to acknowledge that wives, on some occasions, do the same thing.

What should the salesman have done?

AVOIDING THE PYRRHIC VICTORY

In keeping with the incident of the frustrated salesman there are some actions he could have taken.

1. He might have apologized to the receptionist. Even though she had misjudged him, a gesture of friendliness to her might have meant an opportunity to help.

2. He should have kept on at his work. If a man quits his job every time he gets frustrated, he may end up with no work to do.

3. He might have gone to the gymnasium or walked the block. Physical exercise is frequently an outlet for an emotional buildup or hostility, and it doesn't hurt anyone else.

4. He could have called his wife and told her about the upset, and she by her sympathetic listening could have helped.

5. One husband after a hard day calls on ahead to his wife, "Honey, I've had a hard day, treat me gently." And a wise wife has told her husband that when she has her apron on back to front she is not in good shape. Communication stands at the heart of a good marriage relationship.

"Hens always attack a weaker bird, but attacking your chick may only foul up your marriage."

GAME 7

SEXUALANTICS

I'M GETTING TIRED, DEAR...
HOW ABOUT YOU...

THE AIM OF THE GAME: To use the variation of masculinity and femininity and individual sex differences as a means of other making undue demands, or coquetish behavior, or claiming one's opponent is animalistic or not abiding by the rules.

SPECIAL SKILLS FOR THIS GAME:
* A capacity to make veiled insinuations of either "frigidity" or "oversexed."
* An aptitude for devising a subtle scheme of sexual rewards and punishments which are handed out when one's opponent pleases the player.
* A bent for making excuses—"I'm tired," "Why don't you just go to bed, I'll come later"—and offering them as if they were the real truth of the matter.
* A capacity to avoid sexual experiences and feign indifference while inwardly having healthy sexual needs.

NUMBER OF PLAYERS: Preferably a game for two play-ers. Others may be involved by reference to their particular performances.

AN EXAMPLE OF THE GAME OF SEXUALANTICS:

A handsome pair, the Joneses.

John, 175 pounds, 6 feet 3, black hair and blue eyes, a grad-uate of the University of Texas with shoulders of a giant, nipped into a waist that could only belong to a physical-fitness buff.

His personality matches his appearance, and his infectious laugh brings a ready response.

Polly, as soft as John is hard—38, 24, 36—she billows and curves with a voluptuous figure that causes men to stop and look and eagerly respond to the sweet smile that spreads across a baby face haloed by lovely blond hair.

They are a couple to turn heads, and many less bountifully endowed people are filled with envy as they watch this young couple holding hands at a party.

But things are not always the way they appear.

John and Polly have a hang-up in their marriage. It centers on the most intimate aspect of a marriage relationship—sex.

When bedtime draws near at night, Polly can always think of a thousand things she must do before retiring. John, whose job leaves him somewhat the worse for wear at the end of the day, likes to get off early.

When John tells Polly how tired he is, she urges him to get off to bed bright and early and get in a good night's rest.

What Polly does not understand, or appears not to under-stand, is that John has some pressing sexual needs which are in many ways more important than his requirements for sleep and rest.

John often wonders about Polly. She is attractive and inviting

SEX FOR NON-SEXUAL REASONS

Some recent investigators have shown that although sex is a primary biological urge it can be affected by other drives in the personality.

* Some people feeling unloved and unwanted may engage in sexual experiences as a means of obtaining love.

* A person who feels lonely and isolated may see sex as a way of establishing a relationship and thus use it as a defense against loneliness.

* An individual who feels uncertain and inferior may indulge in sex because it gives her a sense that she is needed and of some importance.

* Some people use sex as a demonstration of power and find fulfillment in their partner's submission in the experience.

* A sexual orgasm has a strong element of discharge of tension and sex may come to be sought as a release from anxiety.

* As they rebel against their parents, some young people make a gesture of defiance by violating their parents' sexual standards.

* A wife may use sex as a means of reward and punishment to be bestowed upon her husband when he pleases or displeases her.

* A husband may avoid sexual experiences as he tells his spouse nonverbally that he doesn't really need her.

to him, yet seems to have some real inhibitions about their sexual relations.

If he could look inside Polly's mind, he would discover she is no prude. In her anxiety she has read many books on the subject. But despite all this information she has a rather special attitude towards sex. Like so many women she is aware that sex is a part of a total love experience, but only a part.

Polly wants sex, but only as the culmination of an experience of affection and concern. Because of John's imperious urges, she sometimes wonders within herself whether John is "using" her.

Such a thought is really far from John's mind. Rather impulsive by nature, he sees himself as a pretty good lover. In his mind he imagines that women are looking for a masterful man who will take them over, sweep them off their feet as they sink in grateful surrender.

In actual fact Polly wants anything but that. Within herself she says, "I sometimes wish we could have a good old evening of necking. That he would take time to talk with me first, then let me feel his protecting arms, just hold me, but the moment he feels me close, it's into bed."

When John becomes aggressive, it worries Polly. If she doesn't respond, John's good nature slips and he makes some veiled statements about her frigid nature.

It frequently happens that after one of these episodes Polly will sit down and rethink her situation. She realizes afresh her spouse's needs and decides to make up for it with him.

She now becomes very affectionate, snuggles up close, and makes some not so subtle advances to John.

Because he is still somewhat resentful, John despite a pretty strong libido urge rejects her approach. He insists that he doesn't need sex and he can manage without her.

The episode leaves Polly frustrated, humiliated, and not a little fearful.

INSTANT REPLAY

Polly has had one of those hectic days when everything seemed to go wrong.

Her turn had come for volunteer work at the hospital. Not

only was she late but she found the overburdened staff submerged under an avalanche of work. As she tried to keep up with it all, she wondered if the hospital was not preparing the staff for a spell in the psychiatric ward.

Rushing back home for supper she had a flat and it seemed like an eternity before the man arrived from the service station.

She realized that the evening meal, so hastily prepared, was not very appetizing, but she felt that if John complained she would scream.

He not only didn't complain but after the meal was completed he offered to help with the dishes.

As she stacked away the last pot, Polly felt a surge of weariness sweep over her. At that moment when she wished for nothing more than blissful oblivion, John put his arm around her and said with an unmistakably amorous note in his voice, "What will we do now?"

What should Polly reply?

AVOIDING THE PYRRHIC VICTORY

1. Begin with the realization that sex is creative. God said, "Be fruitful and multiply," consequently sex is not dirty but may be one of the noblest functions of the human personality.

2. Recollect that sex is part of a total love experience. The Greeks used three words which show us three angles of a multifaceted love. *Eros* referred to the sexual emotional side of love, *philia,* the companionate aspect and *agape,* the altruistic or giving component of love. Make sure that you love your mate totally and pay at least as much attention to the companionate and giving, as to the sexual element of love.

3. Realize that you have a sexual obligation in marriage.

Paul speaking about this to husbands and wives said, "Defraud ye not one another." Be thoughtful about your spouse's feelings and responses.

4. Read a good book on sex, preferably one written from a Christian perspective. Let this basic physiologial and psychological information be a starting point for a fair and open-minded consideration of sex.

5. Study the differences between masculine and feminine sexual reaction. In general, the woman is usually more slowly aroused, and her passions subside more slowly. The man is usually the opposite. Remember these simple facts of human response and your love life can become more meaningful.

6. Monotony is as deadening in sexual relations as in other areas of life. Don't be frightened to discuss special needs with your spouse.

7. Don't use sex as a means of rewards or punishment.

8. Remember that sexual difficulties are often a symptom of an underlying difficulty. If these basic problems can be worked out, it may be relatively easy to reduce the sexual difficulty.

"The highest and the lowest are always closest to each other in the sphere of sexuality."

                                                                Freud

GAME
8

NOW! I WONDER WHERE
HE IS OFF TO ...

I   SPY

THE AIM OF THE GAME: The successful player constantly searches for clues about his partner's activities, trying to find some action that can be interpreted as unfaithfulness.

SPECIAL SKILLS FOR THIS GAME:
   * The basic requirement is deep, ingrained suspicion.
   * A capacity for interpreting even the most trivial events in such a way that they will confirm the original hypothesis.
   * A certain detective-like ability to ferret out clues that may help to unmask what it is assumed the partner has hidden so carefully.

NUMBER OF PLAYERS: While there are two main contestants, to play the game successfully there will be a number of subsidiary participants who play small but very important parts in the game.

THE WINNING PLAY

"You won't be home for supper after all the trouble I've gone to to fix your favorite shrimp creole?"

Agnes Williams knew she was acting in a childish way, but she didn't care. She was fed up with James.

After the way she had worked for so long carefully preparing the supper, it was just like him to call up and say he wouldn't be home.

But that wasn't Agnes' biggest worry. She and the children would enjoy the shrimp.

What really bothered her was that Jean Gabriel was probably working late with James. She could just see them alone in the office with Jean telling her tales about the struggles of a divorcee without a husband and bearing the responsibility for two small children.

Agnes shook herself out of her reverie. There was her over active imagination at work again. She had nothing to bother about. Jean was cute, brunette, large brown eyes, but in her saner moments Agnes knew she could easily outclass Jean. Moreover Jean had always been friendly with her and never given any indication of an interest in James.

Poor Agnes has been through all this many times before.

Agnes was flattered when James first paid attention to her in her senior year in college.

As their relationship progressed she could not help but notice the envious looks of some of the other girls, and she sometimes wondered about her good fortune that such a handsome man should be interested in her.

Then would come those growing doubts. Perhaps he was just playing her on.

She knew that men looked at life in a somewhat different way from women, but on the occasions that James went away with a group of the boys, she became apprehensive.

After their return, she couldn't bear the banter as they joked about the girls they'd met and James's buddies teased her saying she'd have to keep an eye on that boyfriend of hers.

After their marriage things went very well until James had to go to a convention. Pregnant at the time, it would have been awkward for Agnes to take the trip, but she felt James wasn't terribly upset about going without her.

When he got back, he brought a nice negligee for her and told her how lonely he'd been by himself.

A few nights later as they were eating with John and Nancy Simon, Agnes volunteered the information that James didn't really enjoy conventions.

John smiled and replied, "If he'd spent more time in the sessions and less with that little blonde from Milwaukee, he might have been more involved in it."

James gave a mock cry of dismay, "Now then John you promised that you wouldn't tell if I didn't."

That spoiled the evening for Agnes, and she had a feeling that James was somewhat restrained.

In the car on the way home she lapsed into silence and thought and rethought the incidents of the evening. As they were preparing for bed, she said, "James what did John mean when he mentioned that blonde from Milwaukee?"

"Oh, Honey, he was just joking. You know the way men talk."

"Was there a blonde from Milwaukee?"

"Yes there was this girl in the same discussion group as I, and we spent some time putting the material together for the report. We had a couple of meals together."

The whole situation irked Agnes and she felt that the very

fact that John commented on it showed there was something in it. Whenever conventions were mentioned, the image of the Milwaukee blonde flashed into her mind.

Then there was that tour when Mrs. Spencer took a shine to James.

They saved so carefully for this tour to England and had to work frantically making arrangements for the children that, by the time they arrived at the airport, Agnes felt as if she needed to go to bed for a week rather than set off on a tour.

Mrs. Spencer was older than they. Much older Agnes thought; James on the other hand felt she had probably married very young. Her husband had died six months before and Joe Lyn Spencer frequently lamented the loneliness of widowhood and would forever persist in telling Agnes how fortunate she was to have such a wonderful husband as James.

In many ways that tour turned out to be a nightmare for Agnes, and the haunting ghost was Joe Lyn Spencer, who seemed to spend a good proportion of her time thinking up things for James to do.

"Will you please help me with this package?"

"I'm sorry Agnes doesn't feel too well; you'll just have to look after me on this side trip."

Agnes had heard about these widows, they knew all the tricks. All the time they were away on that side trip Agnes could see her hanging on James's arm as they climbed the steps, leaning on his shoulder in the bus, and using all her wiles to implicate him.

Both Agnes and James joined the church choir and although a little reluctant at first, James soon found it particularly interesting. No Caruso, he had a pleasing voice, but his main asset was that he related well to the other members of the choir. The

> ## JEALOUSY
>
> **"O jealousy thou magnifyer of trifles."**
>
> **Schiller**
>
> **"The ear of jealousy heareth all things."**
>
> **Apocrypha**
>
> **"Jealousy in a lover is never without an infantile root or at least an infantile reinforcement."**
>
> **Freud**
>
> **"There is more self love than love in jealousy."**
>
> **La Rochefoucauld**

minister of music frequently remarked on how he was good for their morale.

When Agnes felt that the demands of her family were such that she could not continue with choir, the minister of music said, "Agnes, I hate this but I certainly hope it doesn't mean James is going to quit."

So she urged James to stay with the choir.

How often she regretted that move. Marjorie Smith, whose husband had no interest in church, was always at choir, and whenever her car battery went flat, or she ran out of gas, or she was called to the hospital, it would be John who'd help her.

On Thursday nights it seemed as if those two-hour choir rehearsals took an eternity. If James was not home by 9:15, Agnes went through purgatory.

The moment he came in through the door she pounced on him and bombarded him with a barrage of questions: "Where have you been? What kept you? Did Marjorie need some help again?"

INSTANT REPLAY

Agnes is sitting with her friend Jean drinking coffee. They have been talking about the children, rising prices, and the normal problems that beset today's housewife.

Suddenly Agnes bursts into tears: "Oh, Jean, I've just got to talk to someone. I'm so upset. For sometime I've been worried about James."

"It seems as if he always has to be working late these days and that Jean Gabriel, his secretary, has to be with him. I've been worried about it for some time now."

"Last week they had to work late, and about nine o'clock I called the office and the janitor answered. He said there was nobody there; they had all gone home."

"James finally came in at 10:30."

"You know how much I worry about James, I've told you before."

"What should I do?"

What would you tell Agnes?

AVOIDING THE PYRRHIC VICTORY

1. Jealousy isn't always a sign of an individual's love for another person. Fenichel suggests, "The most jealous persons are those who are not able to love but who need the feeling of being loved." The whole experience may really indicate that the individual has an excessive self love.

2. Search your own motivations. Projected jealousy may be an indication that the jealous person has violated his own values and sees his own faults and failures in his spouse or feels his spouse's failure may be a punishment.

3. Women have to be particularly careful. Margaret Mead

PUT AND TAKE IN MARRIAGE

One of the oldest games is called, "put and take" and strange though it may seem the principles of put and take apply to the games husbands and wives play.

Marriage is a two-way street. If it is to be a success, both partners must become involved in the process of putting and taking, especially putting.

As an exercise, sit down and mark off two sheets of paper. Let both husband and wife fill out a separate sheet.

PUT	TAKE
What I am willing to contribute to this marriage.	What I would like to get from this marriage.

After you have completed this exercise. change papers. Think it over for a couple of days. Then arrange a time when you can sit down for a period together.

Can you come to a compromise arrangement?

says that they are called the "jealous" sex, but it might be more accurate to call them the "insecure" sex. Many a woman's economic well-being is dependent on a male, and so she is relatively easily threatened by a rival who might snatch away her security.

4. Give your spouse the benefit of the doubt. A good relationship is built on mutual trust.

GAME 9

WELL! YOU'RE NOT SO GREAT YOURSELF...

OPENNESS

THE AIM OF THE GAME: To attack your spouse under the guise of being "frank" and "open."

SPECIAL SKILLS FOR THIS GAME:
* A certain self-righteous attitude.
* A way of speaking which indicates, "This is going to hurt me more than it hurts you."

NUMBER OF PLAYERS: Generally two.

THE WINNING PLAY

Betty and Charlie Johnson take their family life seriously. So seriously in fact that an unbiased observer might conclude that the constant processes of examination and reexamination of their marital relationship might be rather like a child who had planted a young shrub and periodically dug it up to see what progress it was making.

It sometimes seemed as if they tried almost too hard.

After they had been to a discussion group where the subject under consideration was "openness," they returned home with a firm resolve to really try "openness" as a way of life.

Children safely tucked into bed, Betty and Charlie sat down for their first session.

Betty: "I don't know whether I have ever told you, but I just love the way you are wearing your hair these days. When I first met you, I loved your crew cut. It made you look so athletic.

"I'll never forget the way those girls used to swoon over you. I sometimes found it difficult to believe that you were really in love with me.

"And the passing years have only confirmed my original judgment. I'm so proud of my hubby."

Charlie: "Sweetheart, you overwhelm me. I'm afraid you must look at me through rose-colored glasses.

"When you talk about college days, my mind goes back to the cutest little coed on the campus. I'll never forget that sweater-blouse combination you used to wear.

"You know having children has improved you, Mrs. Johnson. From being a cute little coed you have moved naturally into blooming motherhood."

And so it went on.

Betty and Charlie spent their evening trying to think up nice things to say about each other to the extent that it made them pay attention to their spouse's strong points and it had a certain value.

But it wasn't openness.

Ten days later the Johnsons sat down again to try "openness." In a frank discussion they both admitted that their first session was somewhat forced, stilted, and difficult, and rather than being open they had scrupulously avoided the experience and engaged in mutual admiration.

They decided the situation called for a much franker approach.

Charlie led off, "Honey if we are going to be open, I think I should tell you that there is a little habit of yours that bothers me."

"Oh."

"I can tell by the way you said, 'Oh,' that you really don't want me to tell you."

"Yes I do. Please proceed and let me know."

"Well you are always late. It doesn't matter where we go, I have to stand around and wait for you."

"Is there anything else?" Betty's voice is becoming just a trifle harsh.

"Now, Honey, it's only an experiment with a type of reaction that we hoped would improve our marriage."

"Yes I know. Keep on."

"Well, there is another matter."

"Yes."

"It's the way you interrupt when I'm talking. You know the other night when I was telling the story about fishing at the lake."

"Well you mentioned me. And beside that you had the facts wrong."

"Yes, but I was telling the story and you butted in and spoiled it all."

"All right then, let me tell you a thing or two.

"If you didn't leave me all the work and the sole responsibility for dressing the children, I wouldn't be late. Why most self-respecting husbands wouldn't think of leaving everything to their wives while they sat around and read the paper."

Betty paused trying to blink back the tears that were coming to her eyes.

CONFESSION

As soon as man was capable of conceiving the idea of sin, he had recourse to psychic concealment. Or, to put it in analytical language, repressions arose. Anything that is concealed is a secret. The maintenance of secrets acts like a psychic poison which alienates their possessor from the community. . . .

However beneficial a secret shared with several persons may be, a merely private secret has a destructive effect. It resembles a burden of guilt which cuts off the unfortunate possessor from communion with his fellow beings. Yet if we are conscious of what we conceal, the harm done is decidedly less than if we do not know what we are repressing or even that we have repressions at all. In the latter case we do not merely keep a content consciously private but we conceal it even from ourselves. It then splits off from consciousness as an independent complex to lead a separate existence in the unconscious where it can be neither corrected nor interfered with by the conscious mind. The complex is thus an autonomous portion of the psyche which, as experience has shown, develops a peculiar fantasy-life of its own.

In keeping the matter private . . . I still continue in my state of isolation. It is only with the help of confession that I am able to throw myself into the arms of humanity freed at last from the burden of moral exile.

C. G. Jung

"For him who confesses, shams are over and realities have begun; he has exteriorized his rottenness."

William James

"I was trying to help you when you were telling that story."

Charlie sees the danger signals and suggests they have probably had enough for the night and it might be a good idea if they watched TV for a while before going to bed.

INSTANT REPLAY

Instead of one replay we will try five on this theme. The idea is to take five responses interpreted by some people as "openness' and discover the principles of such an experience.

Replay One

"I don't know why it always happens to me, everything goes wrong with me, that is why I . . . "

Principle. *Openness is not complaining.*

Many people "confess" by bewailing life's misfortunes. This will only make them feel sorry for themselves and accomplish nothing. Giving a long speech about how we feel does little. We really should focus on the way we've been acting.

Replay Two

"I certainly made a big mistake, but my husband was really the cause of it all."

Principle. *Openness is not blaming someone else.*

The natural reaction to defeat is to look around for some scapegoat, and we can easily find someone else to blame. The continued process of blaming others will only raise the level of our own irresponsibility. In a true experience of openness, I acknowledge my own failure.

Replay Three

"When Jim Harris and I went off on our escapade . . . "

Principle. *We do not become open for somebody else.*

Probably the worst type of confession is that which either literally or by innuendo is aimed at advertising someone else's shortcomings. Work on your own personal failures. You have more than enough to discuss before you start on someone else's.

Replay Four

"I want to stand up in church and tell everybody."

Principle. *We only become open before "significant others."*

Probably no single consideration has hurt the idea of openness more than this. Public confession seldom accomplishes any real purpose. We only confess to the person involved or to a committed group of "significant others."

Replay Five

"I guess my main problem is that I try too hard to help other people. While I was trying to help this girl. . . "

Principle. *Boasting is not being open.*

Some people turn virtues into vices. Situations where the individuals were too sweet or too kind are not really confessions.

AVOIDING THE PYRRHIC VICTORY

1. Look at the positive aspects of openness. When a man and his wife live in such a close relationship they should not have large areas of experience which they hide from each other.

2. Surely there must come a time when we sit down and say to our mate: "Honey, you have a right to know who you married. Let me tell you about myself."

3. One of the most reprehensible uses of openness is to utilize it as a means of attack. "Yes, this is what I did but the reason I did it was that you were so cold to me," is not honesty, it is attack.

4. Let us be honest about ourselves without excuse or justification. When we have made a mistake, admit it.

5. Two parties must play their parts in the process—no one should ever sit in judgment on anybody else.

6. Remember the rules of openness:
   (1) Openness is not complaining.
   (2) Openness is not blaming others.
   (3) Openness is not talking about other people's problems.
   (4) Openness is not boasting but talking about our weaknesses.
   (5) Openness takes place with "significant others."

"A man is never stronger than when he is admitting his weaknesses."

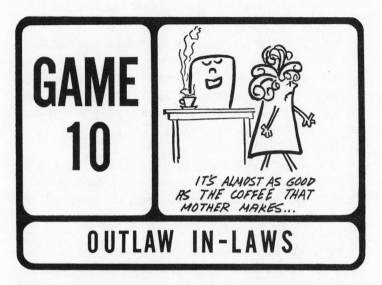

GAME 10

OUTLAW IN-LAWS

IT'S ALMOST AS GOOD
AS THE COFFEE THAT
MOTHER MAKES...

THE AIM OF THE GAME: To hold a strong loyalty to your parents and in maintaining this posture alienate your spouse.

SPECIAL SKILLS FOR THIS GAME:
* Convince yourself that your parents have been so good to you that they deserve your basic loyalty.
* Give your partner the impression that your parents come first and your spouse in second place.

NUMBER OF PLAYERS: A game for four to six players. This number includes a husband and wife and their respective parents.

THE WINNING PLAY

Mrs. Farrel worried over Horace. In her heart lurked an awful apprehension that he might make the wrong move. When he went off to college, she anticipated a multitude of possibilities

—drinking, gambling, drugs, girls, all passed in a parade before her mind.

At times she worried that he was becoming too much involved with some of the designing females who surrounded him. On the other hand when he paid no attention to girls, suspicions of inversion flitted into her mind.

Then came Gloria!

When Horace called to say he had met the one girl in the world for him, Mrs. Farrel could hardly wait to meet Gloria.

And Gloria made a hit. Especially with Mr. Farrel. Perhaps because they didn't have a daughter he was particularly susceptible to girls. As soon as she was introduced to Mr. Farrel, Gloria snuggled up to him, and, as his wife later reminded him, Joe Farrel beamed as broadly as if someone had just given him a million dollars.

In later years Horace wondered at the reception his parents had given Gloria. It seemed almost too good to be true.

The marriage was the supreme moment—for Mrs. Farrel.

Horace and Gloria both wanted to keep things simple, but Mrs. F. realized this was a once in a lifetime event and they should not spare any effort to make it a memorable affair. When at last all the celebrations were concluded, Mrs. F. heaved a sigh of relief but a relief overridden by a sense of achievement.

Mr. Farrel, Horace, and Gloria survived miraculously, but Mrs. Farrel collapsed and had to take to her bed for a week. But she was buoyed up with the knowledge that her son's wedding had gone down as one of the events of Cisco's year.

Horace and Gloria settled in their new little home and gratefully acknowledged all the kindnesses that their in-laws lavished upon them. Gloria's parents lived on a moderate income and some distance away, consequently they could not do much to help the young couple get their new home underway.

Perhaps conscious of Gloria's family's limited means, the Farrels redoubled their efforts to help. They came to light with some money to assist with the deposit on the new house, and periodically ransacked their house for furniture they no longer needed, hoping to provide at least a minimum of furnishings for the new home. The older and younger Farrel families worked together to keep everything going.

And this was the way it went.

It got to be a family ritual that Horace and Gloria would have Sunday dinner with the Farrels and the Farrels in turn made it something of a habit to drop by on Thursdays for supper.

Mrs. Farrel proudly told her friends and neighbors how happy she was that they were so close to their son and their daughter-in-law.

Of course there were a few little things that bothered Mrs. Farrel. That darling Gloria wasn't quite the precise housekeeper Mrs. Farrel would have liked her to be. When she went into their house, she couldn't resist the temptation to straighten up some things and would occasionally drop a pointed hint about how easy it was to keep things neat and tidy.

Mrs. Farrel frequently brought food on Thursdays and generally hurried into the kitchen where she took over, urging Gloria to just take it easy for a while. When they returned home on Thursday nights, Mrs. Farrel had so many stories to tell Mr. Farrel about the way that darling Gloria muddled around in the kitchen and how she had to salvage the meal or they would never have eaten at all.

The arrival of the first child proved to be a happy event. Mrs. Farrel really went into action. The Farrel home became a sort of command post from which the indomitable Mrs. Farrel checked up on Gloria's weight, the doctor's attention, the hospital arrangements, and the insurance coverage.

Her plan for getting Gloria to the hospital was a rival to the U.S. Early Warning System.

She moved Gloria and Horace into her home and did not leave that daughter-in-law alone for one single moment.

In that period of time she only slept lightly and lived in constant anticipation of a nightmare ride to the hospital following a police car with sirens blaring.

The whole event proved to be somewhat anticlimactic. Just one day before the doctor's projected date, Gloria had her first pains at 8 P.M. Horace helped her into the car, she calmly checked into the hospital, and the baby was uneventfully born at five the following morning.

After her discharge from the hospital, Gloria insisted on going to her own house. Mrs. Farrel wanted to have them in the Farrel residence then planned to move over with Horace and Gloria. Gloria thanked her mother-in-law while firmly insisting that they didn't have enough room in their house. She could manage alone.

Mrs. Farrel fluttered around the new baby like some guardian angel. She knew that Gloria was young and not very knowledgeable in the ways of motherhood. She wanted to give that daughter-in-law the benefit of all her own years of experience.

Under the weight of all this attention, Gloria began to harden. Mrs. Farrel's well-intentioned advice grew more and more irritating as time went on.

The climactic moment started unobtrusively enough.

Those Sunday dinners at Farrels particularly irked Gloria.

After dinner they usually put the baby down to nap and dishes done, Horace and his father retired to television while Gloria, left with Mrs. Farrel, listened to a long recital of all the events that had transpired in her mother-in-law's life during the past week.

Evelyn Duvall claims that there are some old wives' tales about mothers-in-law that are wrong. She has made six specific corrective statements:

1. Mother-in-law is not always a curse; oftentimes she is a real blessing.

2. People do not always find it impossible to live with or near their in-laws; many do so and like it.

3. Men are not more frequently annoyed by their in-laws than are women; quite the contrary.

4. Parents-in-law are not more critical of their children's spouses than the other way around; it is the younger generation that is the more critical.

5. Keeping quiet about in-law problems is not the only way to deal with them; many people prefer clearing up their differences as they arise.

6. A person need not feel helpless about his in-law relationships; there is a great deal that can be done to make them satisfactory.

The afternoon dragged on. They frequently stayed so long that it meant having supper with the Farrels. Getting away was like a surgical procedure to separate Siamese twins. Gloria frequently fumed within herself that the only day that they ever had together as husband and wife had to be spent at his mother's place.

All day Monday Gloria laid her plans but when the moment came it wasn't very much like the way she had rehearsed it all.

The supper over, baby fed and bedded down, Horace settled into his favorite chair to watch television.

Imagine his surprise when Gloria walked over, switched off the set and announced, "Honey, I want to talk with you."

"Good," he replied, although he was just a mite upset at

suddenly being divorced from his program. "What do you want to talk about?"

"Well, Honey, it's Sunday dinner."

"Sunday dinner?"

"Yes, I'm sick and tired of going to your mother's for dinner."

"But Honey, I thought you enjoyed going over there and you know it helps our budget and Mother would be very disappointed if we didn't go. You know how she looks forward to it."

"Disappoint your mother! I'm sick to death of your mother. I can't do anything without your mother.

"Why did you ever bother to get married?

"Why didn't you just decide to be a mama's boy and spend all your days living to please her?"

INSTANT REPLAY

You are Horace Farrel's employer. For some time now you have been noticing his apparent lack of interest in his work.

One morning he comes in to see you and says he wants a transfer to a branch office in another state even though it means a lower salary and a move to more limited opportunities.

You push him about his reasons for wanting a transfer, and he tells you about his domestic situation.

Would you help him transfer?

What other counsel would you give?

AVOIDING THE PYRRHIC VICTORY

1. If you want to win the victory in the in-law game, begin with a realization that the husband-wife relationship is basic. It is more important than your relationship with your parents or your children.

2. It is seldom wise to live in the same home as your or your

spouse's parents nor is it a good idea to live too close to them. You need to have time to get to know your spouse and build your relationship and a good portion of this needs to be done away from any possible interference.

3. While many of your in-laws' ideas and practices might irritate you, don't let this blind you to their good points. The old stereotype of mothers-in-law is not always true.

4. Be careful about talking to any relative about your spouse. If you have something to tell your partner, tell him or her not somebody else.

5. There is an old story about a husband who looked at his wife's biscuits and said, "You don't fix biscuits the way Mother used to."

His wife replied, "And you don't bring home the sort of dough that Daddy did."

Holding our parents up as examples is a futile procedure.

6. Try to understand your in-laws. They have some strong points and can be wonderful friends if you keep the relationship intact. Remember you will probably be an in-law yourself one day. Put yourself in their place.

7. Be Christian in this as in all areas of life. The same Bible that tells us to leave our parents and cleave unto a spouse tells us to be kind, affectionate, and long-suffering.

"Behind every successful man there stands an astonished mother-in-law."

GAME
11

YOU THINK YOU HAD A
HARD DAY... WELL! LET ME
TELL YOU....

BLOW-UP

THE AIM OF THE GAME: To gain release from the pressures of life by letting fly with an outburst which is seen as a way of reducing tension.

SPECIAL SKILLS FOR THIS GAME:
* A deep conviction that emotions build up and **must** find some kind of release.
* An ability to let fly without any concern for what damage you might do to anybody else.

NUMBER OF PLAYERS: Any number can play but there are two main contestants in a marriage encounter.

THE WINNING PLAY

Barbara Jackson had majored in psychology because, as she told her parents, it meant that she could go in a number of directions later, guidance, counseling, industrial work. If she just settled down to be a housewife, the courses she had taken in

82

developmental, child, and adolescent psychology would help her to be a better wife and mother.

On a certain Tuesday morning Barbara caught herself reflecting on those days of easy confidence and wondering if the psychology courses might have been nothing more than a mere waste of time.

She well recollected her professor as he said, "And after all our theorizing about motivation and behavior there is always the factor of individual differences."

She could certainly say amen to that!

Those children of hers were such a mixture. Introvert, extrovert, ambivert, she had a sample of each of them in that brood of hers.

What a day this had been!

It all began, as these days so often do, with a bad start. When the alarm sounded out its imperious summons, Stewart reached over and switched it off.

They slept late and breakfast became one mad scramble.

Not only was it the day for the car pool, but just before she left, Mrs. Wickersham called to say she had wrecked her automobile and could not take Nancy to her school, which lay on the opposite side of the town from Barbara's car pool responsibility.

She rushed in turn to those widely separated spots mentally speculating as to the stupidity of placing schools at such great distances from each other.

Breathless and already not a little jittery, Barbara pulled into her driveway and rushed in to answer the demanding telephone.

The school nurse's voice at the other end of the line conveyed a note of urgency. Nancy was sick and, although she didn't yet have a high fever, it would be a good precautionary measure to take her to the doctor.

Into the car and off to the school.

She carefully bundled Nancy in a warm blanket and headed out for the doctor's office inwardly recalling the good old days of doctors' house calls.

Once situated in the crowded waiting room Nancy showed signs of improvement. Barbara tried desperately not to have a suspicious mind but she could not help but think that once Nancy had been reprieved from school her illness was rapidly dissipating.

By the time they got in with the doctor Barbara began to wonder why ever on earth that panicky nurse had called her in the first place.

The doctor examined Nancy in a stony silence then muttered something about "virus," "a lot of this going around now," and with wisdom suggested, "Give her a couple of aspirin and keep her warm. She should be able to go to school tomorrow."

Barbara had determined to show up at the women's club meeting. They were electing officers and she wanted to see Claire Kattinger chosen as program chairman. While waiting at the doctor's, she carefully laid her plans and hurried down to Mrs. Harris to ask her to look after Nancy for a couple of hours.

That 1:30 meeting proved to be a disaster. After the presentation of the slate of officers Barbara got to her weakening feet to move that Claire be a second nominee for program chairman. The president looked at Barbara as if a Benedict Arnold had crept into their midst, and Claire, looking quite different from when she had visited Barbara and hinted that she would like the job of organizing the programs, struck the final blow by withdrawing her name.

Barbara stayed around after the meeting. As much as she needed to go, she didn't want to give the impression of being

---

EMOTIONAL EXPRESSION

Many theories of helping people in psychotherapy are built on the idea that the difficulty may lie in the individual's unexpressed emotions. These emotions have built up blockages which immobilize the sufferer's intellectual capacities. Therefore, the reasoning goes, if we can provide some way in which he can release his emotions he will be able to use his intellectual powers and work on his problem.

With this objective in mind psychotherapists have devised many techniques for releasing emotion. Play therapy, psychodrama, and similar methods help the individual have a catharsis experience, an abreaction, and so drain off the troubles of emotion.

But there are other theories about the neurosis which see the emotional reaction as a "symptom" rather than the cause of the trouble. Focusing on the symptom may only lead us away from the troublesome cause.

The ventilation of emotions may not really be as therapeutic as we sometimes imagine.

---

frightened. All too vividly aware of many of the club members' negative reactions, she brazened it out and stayed twenty minutes longer than she'd intended.

Nancy meanwhile had new accessions of spirit and strength, and when Barbara picked her up and took her home the distracted mother had a few moments in which she seriously considered hog-tying her offspring.

With waves of weariness sweeping over her, Barbara set out on the task of collecting the children in her car pool and delivering them to their homes. After a brief glimpse to make sure that Nancy hadn't wrecked the house, Barbara set out for the supermarket. Anxieties again. Worrying over prices and an interminable line at the check-out stand, and just to finish it off, trying to get out she crumpled the fender of the car.

Blissfully unaware of Barbara's day, Stewart came in full of good spirits. He greeted Barbara with, "What, no dinner ready, whatever on earth have you been doing all day?"

For Barbara this was the last straw. She blew her top. In this moment she recollected his thoughtlessness, his laziness, his stinginess, and she let him have it as clearly as she could.

What Stewart considered a vicious and unwarranted attack chased away every vestige of his good spirits. If that was the way she wanted it, it was OK with him. He responded in like manner and demanded to know why he couldn't ask a simple question without getting his head bitten off.

It is better that a veil be drawn over the rest of that night.

INSTANT REPLAY

Two days later Barbara and Stewart were trying to put things back together again. After Barbara filled him in on the happenings of that horrible day, Stewart could see the reason for it all.

Barbara, the psychology major, gave a final summation of it all, "Well as bad as that episode was there was really a good side to it all. Goodness only knows what might have happened to me if I hadn't been able to get it off my chest."

She gave Stewart that cute little wink he loved so much. "You wouldn't want an emotional cripple on your hands would you? When emotion builds up it's like water behind a dam and it has to be released."

Imagine that you are a psychologist and Stewart has come to you. After relating both the incident and Barbara's interpretation, he says, "Do you think we must express our emotions? Did Barbara go about it the right way?"

AVOIDING THE PYRRHIC VICTORY

1. We cannot just live at the impulse level. Durant says, "The control of impulse is the first principle of civilization." Undisciplined impulses can lead us on a destructive pathway.

2. Many people not only don't find release by an emotional explosion but actually get madder because of the experience. For them the expression stimulates yet more intense emotional reaction.

3. One of the difficulties in expressing emotion is that even if we get relief we frequently hurt someone else in the process. So our release comes at the expense of injuring someone else and this is often someone we love.

4. Life must not be lived simply at the emotional level. There are other considerations, such as responsibility.

5. If we learn to act right we may be surprised to discover how our feelings follow our action.

6. If you have to vent your emotions, play golf, work out in the gym, or undertake some form of physical activity which will not involve someone else on the receiving end.

"Anger is momentary madness, so control your passion or it will control you."

Horace

GAME
12

DON'T LET ME INTERRUPT,
DEAR... BUT...

SNATCH THE BALL

THE AIM OF THE GAME: To make sure that you are constantly speaking.

SPECIAL SKILLS FOR THIS GAME:
* The ability to "tune out" your mate when he or she is speaking.
* To be alert for an opportunity to correct or supplement your partner's statements.
* Develop a capacity to anticipate a momentary lag in conversation and then jump in and change the subject.
* Complete oblivion to the feelings of other people linked with a lack of concern for our relationship with them.

NUMBER OF PLAYERS: Any number can play.

THE LOSING PLAY

"Did I have a time learning to use these things."

Like some conductor about to bring his orchestra into its

crashing crescendo, Ed Simpson waved not one, but two batons, as he proudly sliced the air with a pair of ivory chopsticks.

With an ease obviously born of much thought and practice, Ed held forth on the art of using chopsticks. "You hold the bottom stick stationary between the middle and ring fingers at one end and between the base of the thumb and index finger at the other end. You hold the top stick between the thumb, index, and middle fingers, as if it were a pen."

He displayed a remarkable expertize as he seized on an imaginary piece of sweet and sour pork, or ladled rice from an equally impalpable dish, at an incredible speed.

The group of men standing in the surrounding circle responded politely, and Ed felt like some archaeologist newly returned from years of research in the arid wastes, bearing in his hand a rare artifact, only to find a sophisticated populace singularly unimpressed.

For Ed and Lois their trip to the Orient had been the culmination of a lifelong dream. They had planned and saved for it for so long and now having returned they were anxious to relive every golden moment.

So they had invited all their friends to come for the evening. The trinkets and mementoes were carefully displayed. A Japanese paper fan was wrapped for each guest.

Ed had nearly driven the camera store mad. On the trip he'd used his camera like a tommy gun, in rapid succession firing off pictures of everything that came in sight. Now he chafed at the time it took to get all the pictures back and worked for hours at sorting and selecting.

He could hardly believe it when the man at the store suggested one hundred slides were enough for an evening's showing. With nearly nine hundred pictures processed, this news sent him into the agonizing process of deciding what precious pictures could be eliminated. A blind man could see their uneven quality, but those under or over exposed generally had some story that made it absolutely essential that he retain them.

Many hours before the guests arrived, Ed set up the screen and the projector with the magazines of slides ready.

Lois had earlier lectured Ed about not screening the pictures too early, and while he could see some reason for this, he had a grim suspicion that she was anxious to show off her new knit dresses, her watch, those pearls, and sundry other items.

"Come on everybody, gather around, we're not in Japan where they segregate the women from the men." Lois, tired of waiting for Ed to finish his chopstick demonstration to the circle of men, moved into action even though she noted the look of disappointment spreading over her husband's face.

Determined to involve him, she announced: "We want everybody to hear what Ed has to tell us, but I think we've had enough of the chopsticks. Now Ed, why don't you tell us about the trip over in the plane."

Ed recovered his confidence, "Well I don't mind telling you, you haven't lived until you've traveled on a Japanese airline."

He paused as if refreshed by the memory of it all. "As soon as the plane takes off, these cute hostesses in kimonos came around with hot towels."

"But Honey," Lois had moved in to have her say, "The Thai airlines not only provide hot towels, but they give each woman an orchid as she comes on board."

"Well," Ed had lost his momentum and struggled to pick it up again.

Lois had set the pattern for the evening.

When Ed told them about the wonderful camera buys in Hong Kong, it reminded Lois of bargains in sweaters. As he

THE CONVERSATION GAME

Conversation itself can be a delightful game which you can learn to enjoy and at the same time help others. Some simple ground rules are:

1. Don't talk about yourself. Like a seasoned tennis player who is trying to help the beginner and gently lobs the ball in front of him so that it will be easy for him to hit, try to turn the flow of interchange into areas of your partner's interests.

2. Don't dominate the conversation. Remember discussion is a two-way street. Let your partner have a turn and when in doubt give up and let him take over.

3. Avoid side groups. If your spouse is addressing himself to your foursome, fight the temptation to start a side conversation with one of the group. Let him have his moment.

4. Don't make harsh negative statements. Even if you disagree, acknowledge some of the strong points in the statement then lead tactfully around to your point of view.

5. Give evidence of your attention. Don't sit looking at the floor or ceiling or carrying on some other activity. Make it obvious that you are really listening.

6. Keep the conversation on the subject. If there is some interruption or an aggressive member of the party has diverted the conversation, gently draw it back to the original subject.

7. Above all don't interrupt. Remember that conversation is a fine art. Practice constantly to become proficient.

recalled the delights of sukiyaki, she recollected the horror of struggling to eat raw fish, and his account of a Shinto temple caused Lois to break in with a story about the students who washed their mouths after a visit to the temple.

So it went on. Whatever Ed started to tell reminded Lois of some person, unusual custom, or strange event. By the time the evening was over, Ed had the feeling that he'd never had the satisfaction of completing one single story.

In Lois' mind the evening went down as a great event, in Ed's, a colossal failure.

Ed smarted every time he recalled that evening. All the next day his mind periodically returned to what now in reflection he considered a debacle. It haunted him.

By midday he'd made up his mind. There was no sense in bottling it up within him. He'd really have it out with Lois. They needed to settle this issue once and for all. Lois' tendency to butt in and interrupt was really getting to him. They must do something about it.

Ed picked up the phone, called home, and told Lois not to fix supper; he would take her out to eat.

The meal over, as tactfully as he knew how, Ed set about introducing the subject.

"Honey, I planned this evening because I want to have a talk with you about a little matter . . ."

"Sweetheart, that was wonderful of you. I could hardly believe my ears when you called to say you wanted to take me out for dinner. That was such a sweet thing for you to do. I knew you probably realized I was tired out from all the preparations of last night."

Already Ed was beginning to get the feeling he was losing the initiative.

"I really had an ulterior motive. I wanted to be sure we'd be alone. . . ."

"That's what I like about you Ed. Far too many men let the romance go out of their marriage, and I sometimes wondered. You know I was talking to Mary Jones and she told me that Bill never takes her out. As a matter of fact just between you and me, I've never really trusted that Bill—"

Ed had had it. That strange awful sensation that Lois was off again like some maverick steer careering across the range. A horrible hostility began to rise within Ed.

"Honey." Ed surprised himself a little at the way it came out, low so that no nearby eater could hear but intense and laden with emotion. "Will you please stop talking for just one moment."

For once, Lois got the message. "Why, Ed, whatever on earth is bothering you?"

"Lois." Ed always called her Honey and the way he pronounced her name, it almost seemed as if he were saying, "Mrs. Simpson."

"Lois, I'm fed up with your incessant interruption. I sometimes wonder if I have ever completed a statement in all our married life.

"It was just like that party last night. Every time I started to tell something, you just had to jump in and take over."

Poor Lois. She sat there dumbfounded.

Both Ed's intensity and his accusation mollified her. She felt called upon to justify the previous evening's activities. "Why Ed, I'm surprised at you. I was only trying to help you. I thought we were partners in our marriage. As I saw it, it was my wifely responsibility to help you."

Ed recognized a dangerous point in the discussion he'd planned for so long. Inwardly a gnawing, growing suspicion warned that he might have been exaggerating the situation. Don't weaken now, he cautioned himself, or maybe you'll be lost.

"It's one thing to be a partner but another to be so insistent that you never let me finish anything I start to say."

"Ed Simpson, I'm terribly disappointed in you," the tears began to roll down Lois' face.

The sight of those tears finished Ed. Over him swept the realization that he'd been a heel. He reached over and took Lois' hand.

"Honey, I'm sorry. I didn't mean to upset you. Let's forget all about it. I'm just a clumsy male. I'm ashamed of myself. Dry those tears."

Lois dabbed her eyes with her left hand while squeezing Ed's with her right, "Is my makeup all right, or do I need to go to the powder room?"

INSTANT REPLAY

Lois is sitting in the circle of women in the renewal group. Although she had a sense of accomplishment in having maneuvered Ed into a corner in the restaurant, second thoughts came later.

Today she had not been her usual cheery self and she lapsed into an unaccustomed silence.

As the meeting got underway, the leader suddenly turned to Lois. "Lois, I've never seen you so gloomy. Are you facing a problem?"

Lois half smiles, then says: "I certainly am, and I'm hoping someone here today can help me. For once in my life, I'm ready to listen instead of talk."

Out comes the story and at the conclusion, Lois looks at the group and says, "What should I do?"

Imagine you are a member of the group. What would you tell her?

AVOIDING THE PYRRHIC VICTORY

1. Some husbands and wives are positively rude and ill mannered when relating to each other. They interrupt, question, or pour scorn on a partner with only the slightest provocation. Be

at least as courteous to your spouse as you would to someone else you meet in your social circle.

2. One woman claimed an infallible method of discovering the marital status of the other diners in a restaurant. If unmarried, they looked into each other's eyes and talked avidly. If married, they sat in silence working their way through the meal. Don't take your partner for granted.

3. Acknowledge the importance of communication in marriage. The biblical idea of "one flesh" implies there should be open channels between two people made one in matrimony.

4. Face the fact that husbands and wives don't listen to each other. You must work on your "listening inertia" and deliberately and determinedly set about "tuning in" your mate.

5. If the situation has deteriorated, undertake a plan of positive action.

* Settle on a specific time period, say Thursday from 7:00 to 7:30 P.M.

* Arrange for a place where there are no children, no television, and a minimum possibility of interruption.

* If the situation is sensitive, make a division of time: ten minutes for her, ten for him, the rest of the time for exchange.

* Agree there will be no interrupting, no flying off the handle, no sulking.

6. Anything you possess—home, car, television set—requires maintenance. What makes you think your marriage won't get a gremlin in it every now and then? Continue to work at it. Particularly communication. Remember, communication is the lifeline of marriage.

"Listening is the other half of talking."

GAME
13

BUT HONEY, IT
WAS ONLY HALF PRICE!

FUNNY MONEY

THE AIM OF THE GAME: To realize that money is much more than a mere medium of exchange and use it to maneuver and manipulate your spouse.

SPECIAL SKILLS FOR THIS GAME:
* A certain naive attitude towards life that no matter how much money you spend everything will turn out all right in the end.
* A strong streak of suggestibility and willingness to respond to the talk of salesmen and ideas of advertising.
* A deep-rooted conviction that you can take independent action in the area of finances without consulting your spouse.

NUMBER OF PLAYERS: Two main players—husband and wife—certain others—in-laws, salesmen—play subsidiary but significant roles.

96

THE WINNING PLAY

The van moved into the driveway and the driver, parcel under his arm, walked up the pathway to the door of the house. A waiting woman who had obviously been on the lookout, opened the door, took the parcel, and closed the door again.

Hurrying across the room, she headed down the hallway to the bedroom, and with a skill born of long practice pushed the parcel under the bed, rose to her feet, and straightened the bedspread with adept fingers. When she stood back, even the most fastidious housewife could not have told the spread had ever been disturbed.

A plot to plant a bomb? A secret cache of drugs?

No, none of these. Just Mollie Suskin making sure her husband didn't know about the purchases she'd made.

Some people cannot resist alcohol, some tobacco, others dope, but Molly's weakness was in a more mundane area. She just spent more money than the family finances would allow.

The word bargain did something to Molly. Whenever she saw an item "marked down," "reduced," "35 cents off," "usually . . . now . . . ," it sparked some motivation which made the object going cheap highly desirable in her eyes.

It may have come in part from her background. Both her mother and father had always lavished her with her every whim, and they had both warned her about the adjustments she'd have to make when she married Tim. She in turn felt they were exaggerating because they were disappointed in her choice of a future husband.

Tim knew the value of a dollar. He grew up the hard way. His father worked as a mechanic, and every penny had to be rolled on its edge. No fancy spending with them.

From the day they began to plan their marriage Tim continually cringed at the expenditures. At first so grateful when Molly's father said, "Don't worry, Molly will only be married once, we're picking up the tab," he soon began to have second thoughts.

He couldn't help thinking about things they could have bought with what he considered the inordinately large expenditures on the wedding.

No sooner were they set up in their little home than Tim called a halt to the paternalism of Molly's family, which he saw as a threat to his status as husband and head of the house. He insisted that they live on his salary and not take a single penny from her parents.

Molly alternated in her reactions. She hated to hurt her parents but nevertheless had a certain sense of pride as she told them of Tim's decision.

Difficult days followed. Molly had to learn the use of money from the ground up and Tim worked with her in working out a budget. She tried hard but found it very difficult to restrain her spending. The whole budget seemed unnecessarily restrictive.

Then began the bargain binge. It seemed to Molly that whenever she bought something at a price lower than that for which it normally sold, she had saved money.

Tim got to dread Thursday evenings. Molly would seize hold of the paper and systematically, page by page, examine the "weekend specials."

He didn't mind it so much on the groceries. But even in that department Molly could scarcely resist the temptation to overbuy the specials. Whatever on earth did they need with twelve cans of Alaskan King crab? the fish-hating Tim asked himself.

Molly for her part resorted to subterfuge. She developed all

PREPARING A BUDGET

Setting up a budget is going to take time and perseverance, but you will find it rewarding in more than just finances. The following steps will help:

1. Determine your goals. Set up some of these on a long-range basis, some for next year, and others for this year.

2. Estimate your income. Put down how much money will be available and the source from which it will come.

3. Estimate your expenses. Divide these into two groups, the fixed which come around regularly in the same amounts, and the flexible which change in the course of a year.

4. Plan your family spending.

* Make the plan flexible, it will probably have to be changed as time goes on.

* Make the plan fit. The average family is hypothetical. Determine your family's specific needs.

* Put it on paper. This will be a challenge but it will enable you to take an objective view of your financial situation.

* Provide for past unpaid bills. As obnoxious as they seem, they must be paid.

* Plan to save. Don't let all your income slip through your fingers. Try to save from 5 to 10 percent of your take-home pay. Remember Wesley's words, "Earn all you can, save all you can, give all you can."

An excellent planning book, Christian Family Money Management, is available from Stewardship Services, 127 Ninth Avenue North, Nashville, Tennessee 37203.

---

kinds of sneaky ways for covering her tracks, so that Tim wouldn't know the way she had spent the money.

After one painful episode in which Molly finally had to tell Tim about a four hundred dollar expenditure, he really got mad.

In an effort to justify herself Molly countered, "But Honey, it was such a good buy. I just couldn't pass it up."

All effort at self-control abandoned, Tim replied: "A good buy, a bargain. I'm sick to death of having to spend money to save it!

"Who do you think you are? Mrs. Rockefeller?

"It's just getting beyond me. I work all the week and all I ever see is bills, bills, bills."

Molly, overwhelmed by Tim's intensity, dissolved into tears.

When the emotions finally subsided, they sat down and went over the budget agreeing that Tim would sign the checks so that he could keep an eye on their expenditures.

The next six months went fairly well but a number of crisis experiences came and went as they struggled with those finances.

Tragedy struck Molly's family when her father, usually so hale and hearty, without prior warning, suffered a heart attack and died.

But even in death, Daddy had arranged everything. His will was precise. What was to be done with the estate, where his wife was to live, and for his daughter the sum of $60,000.

The initial reaction of Molly and Tim was joy, but Tim noted the money was in a trust and Molly's alone. As soon as he had digested the terms of the legacy, Tim realized the intent of Molly's father and he insisted that he would never benefit in any way from the money.

Molly now free to shop bargains and specials as frequently as her heart desired found the zest had gone out of it all. As she displayed the latest bargain she would anticipate Tim's objection and say, "Don't say it's extravagance, I bought it with *my* money."

They had dreamed about a trip to Europe and had written for pamphlets, brochures, and information. Tim had three

AN APPROACH TO FINANCIAL PROBLEMS

A husband and wife belonged to Alcoholics Anonymous and had their drinking habits under control but were plagued with financial difficulties. So they took the twelve steps of A.A. and applied it to finances, coming up with the following:

1. We admitted we were powerless over money and that our lives had become unmanageable.

2. Came to believe that a power greater than ourselves could restore us to sanity in handling our financial affairs.

3. Made a decision to turn our will and our lives and our financial affairs over to the care of God as we understood him.

4. Made a searching and fearless inventory of our financial condition.

5. Admitted to God, to ourselves, and to another human being the exact nature of our financial behavior.

6. Were entirely ready to have God remove the cause of our being in bondage, in debt.

7. Humbly ask him to remove the cause of our indebtedness.

8. Made a list of all our debts, and became willing to pay in full.

9. Paid off as much as we could and let our creditors know of our intentions.

10. Continued to take inventory daily to remind ourselves of our purpose and remained on guard against new extravagances or negligence.

11. Sought through prayer and meditation to improve our conscious contact with God, praying for power to do whatever we have to to get out of debt.

12. Tried to carry the message to others.

Why not try this?

weeks vacation coming up so Molly saw a golden opportunity.

When Molly made the suggestion, Tim replied that they were going to have to trade the car this year and he didn't see how they could possibly afford a vacation in Europe.

Unthinkingly, Molly came up with what seemed to her to be the simple easy answer. "Honey, why don't we pay for it out of *my* money."

"*Your* money," Tim's voice laden with emotion assaulted Molly's ears.

"I'm sick of your money. If you hadn't inherited that money you'd have never been worth a penny. I've always worked hard for everything I've got and now I'm going to live off you.

"No. I'm sorry. If I never go to Europe I'm not going to let you use *your* money."

INSTANT REPLAY

Mrs. Suskin sat in her daughter's living room. She'd found it difficult to adjust to a new way of life but was gradually getting things under control.

She looked at Molly, "Now, Honey, you take care of that husband of yours. Nothing will ever replace him. Even if he leaves money as your father did, money alone is never enough."

Molly filled with tears. "Oh, Mother, I know that, and I do so desperately want to have a good marriage, but I'm afraid things are not doing so well with Tim and me."

"Honey, I'm sorry. Is there anything I can do?"

"No, Mother, nothing. Please don't try. It seems as if Daddy's effort to help me has backfired. Like leaving me that money. I wish I'd never received it.

"Oh Mother what should I do?"

Put yourself in Mrs. Suskin's place. What would you tell Molly?

AVOIDING THE PYRRHIC VICTORY

1. Every member of the family has his *unlimited dreams*—what we would like to have—colored TV, automobile, home, and so forth. These dreams are fostered by our desires, what other people talk about, the advertising pressures of manufacturers.

2. Despite these dreams, we have *limited funds*—a certain amount of money that we can spend. Some things must be paid for—rent, installments, payroll deductions. What is left over is our "discretionary income," and deciding what to do with this is the crux of the problem.

3. How is the income to be garnered? Will the wife work? If so, make sure you have a clear understanding as to how much money she will "take home," add extra expenses, decide on the division of domestic labor.

4. Try to be as clear as possible about how much "discretionary income" you have. Set up a family budget (see box).

5. Money management is never easy. Witness the number of businesses that go into bankruptcy. The situation is even more complex in the family. Begin by deciding on your priorities. What goods and services are most important to all the members of the family.

6. In marriage all the money belongs to both of you. A joint bank account seems a good idea. Put all the cards on the table. Don't have secret little ventures on the side. You should both know where all the money is going.

7. Who will be the treasurer and pay the bills? Him, her, or both? Decide early and know what is happening.

8. Both husband and wife are entitled to some money of their own so that they don't have to ask for little items that they should be able to buy.

GAME 14

DON'T WORRY, DARLING.
LOVE WILL TAKE CARE OF EVERYTHING.

LOVE GAME

THE AIM OF THE GAME: To base a monogamous, lifetime marriage on a foundation of a fluctuating emotional love experience.

SPECIAL SKILLS FOR THE GAME:
* A special capacity to look at all of life in terms of an emotional reaction.
* Glamorize life so that you don't pay enough attention to working at building the broad base of marriage.
* Refuse to see the part that action plays in working on any good relationship.

NUMBER OF PLAYERS: Two people—husband and wife—play the main parts but children join as do other participants.

THE LOSING PLAY

Arnold Kinsler turned the ignition key and the engine roared into life. Pausing for a moment and looking over at the church from which the family had just exited, he heaved a sigh of relief, "Well we have that over for another week."

"Please Arnold," Harriet's tone of voice shrieked the message that said, "not again . . . not in front of the children."

"Oh, Honey, I was only joking. Rev. Smalskald is quite a fair preacher, but he's not practical enough. He doesn't know what it's like to struggle in the business world and have to fight it out for a living."

Harriet looked straight ahead, determined not to be drawn into the discussion. From long experience she knew how it would go. Arnold who saw himself as the man of reason and logic, remained forever amused by what he considered his wife's sentimentality.

Yet that romantic streak in Harriet had attracted Arnold to her in the first place.

They attended the same college; and while Arnold criticized the poor quality of a professor's teaching, Harriet would only comment that his nose was cute or he wore such nice clothes or he had such an attractive wife.

Harriet's mind was peopled with strong men and sweet women and cuddly children. Arnold's with problems, income, and expenditure. In response to her statement that marriages were made in heaven, he reminded her that they were living on earth.

They were both smitten pretty badly, and when Arnold suggested they should get married, her immediate response was, "Do you really love me?"

Flowery phrases didn't come easily to Arnold, but Harriet insisted that he declare his love and that he periodically repeat it. But even after his specific declaration of love and affection, Arnold would insist they must frankly face the mundane facts of living—costs, insurance, and mortgage payments.

"Yes, I know," his spouse would reply, "but love is the important factor. No matter what difficulties we encounter love will find a way."

He grew to enjoy some of those sweet, uncritical, ridiculous statements that she made. Then he'd come in with a realistic matter-of-fact statement that would demolish her dreams to his satisfaction but leave her unconvinced.

On the trip to Florida they stopped at Nashville to visit the Parthenon. To Harriet, with her vivid imagination, it seemed like a trip back into history. Approaching the building she burst into a rapturous statement: "Oh, Arnold, isn't it wonderful? An exact reproduction of the historic building in Athens. I feel as if I ought to be wearing a white gown and sandals with a chaplet on my head."

Amused by her enthusiasm, Arnold tried to look knowing.

Once inside the building Harriet continued to rave on. She paused for a moment then turned to Arnold: "Isn't it wonderful? What are you thinking, Arnold?"

Arnold looked thoughtful and then as if making a profound philosophical declaration responded, "It sure would hold a lot of hay."

"Arnold you are impossible."

Thinking back on that incident Harriet could not help but feel that it dramatized their relationship. Arnold the matter of fact, logical, down to earth; Harriet the eternal romantic.

Following their marriage, Harriet determined that theirs was not going to become one of those humdrum relationships in which they took each other for granted.

Even though Arnold said it wasn't necessary she was up in the morning to get him off to work. When he came through the door in the evening, Harriet, daintily clad in a crisp clean dress, waited to welcome him.

Anniversaries were special affairs. If they didn't eat out, they had an intimate candlelight affair in the protective walls of their own home.

Arnold tried desperately to keep up with it all, but his heart wasn't really in it. He wrote down the dates of Harriet's birthday, their engagement, their wedding, and sundry other times Harriet counted memorable. But he sometimes experienced a vague uneasiness that he had missed something. Could it have been a significant anniversary?

Once when he lost his datebook for a few days he had more concern about those significant dates than the business appointments he might have missed.

"Arnold, Arnold." Out of the mists of sleep in what seemed an early morning hour, he came in response to the summons of his spouse's voice. He wearily opened his eyes to see Harriet sitting up in bed.

"Time to get up."

"Just as well you woke me. I would have overslept."

"Yes and there's a special reason. Do you remember what day it is today?"

Arnold wracked his brain, what was it? Birthday? no. Anniversary? no. PTA meeting?

"I give up, Honey. I can't for the life of me remember it. What is it?"

"You don't remember?" Harriet's countenance took on a cloud of quizzical disappointment.

"No, I don't."

"Well if you don't remember then I'm not going to tell you."

A perplexed Arnold left for work that morning. Several times during the day he puzzled over that pesky event in their lives that called for a special celebration.

The rugged businessman who braved the freeway traffic,

confronted salesmen, and disciplined staff members quaked inwardly at the thought of facing a sweet little 126 pound woman and admitting that he'd forgotten a special event in her life.

Entering the door of their home that night, Arnold Kinsler carried a sleek parcel, beautifully gift wrapped.

Harriet ran to meet him. He enveloped her in his arms and then delivered his carefully prepared speech. "Honey, I'm sorry. I've forgotten what anniversary it is, but I've brought you a new carving knife."

He stood there like some penitent who having made his confession waits for the words of mercy and absolution.

Harriet looking somewhat embarrassed herself replied, "Oh, that's OK. Let's forget all about it. Thank you so much for the knife."

"But what anniversary was it?"

"It wasn't an anniversary at all."

"Not an anniversary?"

"No, it was the day to put out the garbage."

That incident became a family legend to be recounted to every visitor. Arnold declared it would probably be told to their children's children. Yet even as he laughed about it he had a sense of, "That's the stupid situation that all this romantic nonsense gets a man into."

The birth of the twins slowed down Harriet's romantic practices. A difficult pregnancy with spells of morning sickness reduced her enthusiasm for what Arnold somewhat cruelly referred to as "the frills of life."

Following the children's birth it was work, work, work. The frustrated Harriet labored under a burden that pressed down on her with a sense of never having completed all the tasks that should have been finished in any one day.

Looking back on it later Harriet came to see the subtle way in

LOVE IS SOMETHING . . .

Love may be the most misunderstood word in the English language, one of the reasons being that it is an "umbrella" word that includes a number of different meanings. Some languages like Greek have avoided this difficulty with our English word love by using different words to describe different types of love.

"Love is something you feel." The Greeks called this type of love eros. This must be the most widely propagated idea about love. We think of the racing pulse, the excited reaction and we are carried away with the thrill of it all. But emotions are notoriously volatile. They may change from day to day. On this basis love may come and go.

"Love is something you think." One of the Greek words for love, philia, has the idea of companionship. People who think similarly enjoy being together. Their shared interest form the basis upon which a relationship is built. A man's wife, for example, should be his friend.

"Love is something you do." The richest Greek word of all for love is agape which means to give. It is a word of action.

Probably no single book on love has affected so many people as Henry Drummond's Greatest Thing in the World. In this writing he tells us how to learn to love.

"What makes a man a good cricketer: Practice. What makes a man a good artist, a good sculptor, a good musician? Practice. What makes a man a good linguist, a good stenographer? Practice. What makes a man a good man? Practice. Nothing else. . . . Love is not a thing of enthusiastic emotion. It is a rich, strong, manly, vigorous expression of the whole round Christian character—the Christlike nature in its fullest development. And the constituents of this great character are only to be built up by ceaseless practice."

which the twins became her all-consuming passion in life and gradually but surely replaced Arnold. The twins so helpless and needing her, Arnold self-sufficient. Arnold hardheaded and practical, the twins sweet and responsive. People clustered around admiring the twins who soon learned to ham it up, Arnold increasingly obsessed with his business, disinterested in the social and church life Harriet enjoyed so much.

"Your children are only young once," the speaker at PTA had said and Harriet took those words to heart. Her life revolved around her children's activities—school, church, Brownies, Little League, Scouts.

She sometimes wished they'd both been the same sex. A boy and a girl meant doubling up on the intensive activity program. But it had its compensations. You saw both sides of life and met twice as many people.

So it came to pass that Arnold and Harriet gradually but inevitably moved into two separate worlds. Not of intent of course. They just drifted into it.

With his concentrated attention Arnold's business prospered. It needed to. Expenses at home continued to mount, and while Arnold sometimes grumbled about increasing costs he knew that he could manage it nicely.

Then came the blow.

To say the least of it the situation was awkward. Harriet had a jillion things to do in getting the twins ready for camp. Now Arnold called and asked her to meet him at the Golden Ox for dinner. She explained all the reasons why it was impossible for her to get away, but Arnold insisted he had something of the utmost importance to discuss with her and everything else was insignificant. In a rather cutting rejoinder to her statement about the twin's camp he said he didn't care whether the twins got to camp or not.

Convinced, Harriet abandoned all her plans and headed for town.

On that trip, Harriet's mind raced as she inwardly speculated about the cause of such an imperious summons. Amid this confusion of thoughts she could only be grateful that the freeway traffic moved in an almost unbroken line out of town leaving her inbound lanes clear and open.

"Well, Honey, I suppose you are wondering why I insisted that you meet me here." The main course concluded and awaiting dessert, they sat in a secluded corner of the restaurant.

"I certainly am curious. It had better be good. I had all those things to pack for the twins."

"I don't know whether it's good or not, but I'm glad that I outranked the twins for once."

Harriet noted the sarcasm and winced inwardly from a momentary sensation of guilt at the recollection of the order of priorities in her home.

Somewhat apprehensively, but calmly, Arnold continued, "Do you remember how you have always insisted that love was the basis—the only basis—for a good marriage relationship?"

Harriet didn't answer. Arnold continued, "As you know I didn't buy that, I always insisted on a more logical basis for our relationship.

"However after all these years you've finally convinced me. You're right, Harriet. One hundred percent.

"And the reason why I've asked you to meet me here tonight is that without hurting you, I think you are a wonderful mother and housekeeper, I have to be honest with you and tell you I no longer love you. In fact I now wonder if I ever did."

Harriet sat in stunned silence, then spoke: "Oh Arnold, how can you say that. You know the way I've stood beside you all these years and reared your children."

"You've reared my children all right. In fact, they're the only ones you've ever really loved.

"Oh I remember how I laughed at the idea of love but I've gradually worked toward the conclusion that it is the base for marriage. And because of this I can see no reason why we should continue this relationship.

"I've rented an apartment and I'm planning to move out tonight. I'm sorry it had to end this way.

"And there is no sense in trying to hide it all. You'll probably find out. I feel I've discovered the sort of love you've always talked about. I'm sick of just being a meal ticket, and I know a woman who loves me and cares for me."

INSTANT REPLAY

Harriet passed through the greatest tumult of her life. At first she was so hurt that she told Arnold to go ahead and get his divorce. She suggested they act like two sensible adults. As long as he made provision for the twins, she didn't much mind what he did.

In her pain Harriet didn't even try to find out the name of the other person. She inwardly decided she would just concentrate on her children and forget all about Arnold.

A few weeks later she planned to accompany the twins to a social evening at the church, but they both let her know they didn't want Mother along for the evening. Just drop them off at the church and collect them later.

That night as she sat in her lonely house, the foreshadowings of a new kind of life that lay ahead of her began to become clear.

Slowly and painfully, there came to Harriet the awareness that she had had the wrong attitude towards Arnold for many a long year.

When Arnold came in late that night to pick up his golf clubs, he found Harriet waiting up for him. After they'd talked for a while, she said, "It isn't easy for me to say this, it hurts my pride." She paused, then went on, "Arnold I've been a fool. I've done everything wrong. I know it's too late now, but please tell me. I don't want to repeat my mistake. Where did I go wrong?"

What would you say?

AVOIDING THE PYRRHIC VICTORY

1. The basic loyalty in a marriage is not the children. They will someday grow and want their independence leaving their father and mother alone together. The basic human loyalty is that of a wife to her husband.

2. Rougemont, the Swiss scholar, claims that a marriage based solely on romantic love is in a bad condition. Because of the idea that romance implies a relationship that thrives on striving for an unobtainable love object, when marriage brings certainty, it may kill the essential ingredient in romance.

3. Examine the box on "Love Is Something." A good love experience starts with *philia* or companionship, is motivated by *eros,* or emotional love, and must always involve *agape* or giving love.

4. The self-helpers stress the importance of action. "Act as if" they are told. If you act, the rewards will follow. Some of them use the aphorism, "It's much easier to act yourself into a new way of feeling than to feel yourself into a new way of action."

5. Some people feel that if we "act is if" we may be hypocritical, but this is determined by the circumstances. The motivation enters. If we "act as if" to deceive, it is wrong, but if we "act as if" to learn some new way of living, it can be redemptive.

The End of the Game

One theory about play contends that the simple games of early days are preparing the child for life by helping him participate in make-believe situations. As he grows into adulthood, play is relinquished for the realities of life.

We've played fourteen games that led to losses. Each game concluded with a program that would have changed defeat to success.

Have we learned any lessons?

Hopefully some learning has taken place.

If it has, you and your spouse may want to make some new commitment in your marriage.

Look at the Second Marriage Contract.

Read it carefully!

Talk it over!

Think about it!

If you're convinced, you might like to make a new start and begin by "signing up."

OUR SECOND MARRIAGE CONTRACT

I AGREE that I really am interested in preserving our marriage and I will listen to any practical suggestion you have whereby I can improve my conduct toward this goal. I know I am far from perfect, and I will welcome any constructive advice that may help me fulfill myself.

I AGREE to be as honest with both you and myself as I possibly can be. I will withhold no information about my behavior, either before or since we married. You have full right to know the person you married.

I AGREE that I will listen to your remarks and comments without interrupting you. When it is my turn to talk, I expect the same courtesy.

I AGREE that I will first look for things to criticize about myself before I criticize you. Before I complain to you, I will name some fault of mine that, if corrected, would make me a better marriage partner.

I AGREE to cooperate in writing out a list of specific family goals that I am willing to support--and I agree to accept responsibility for doing anything and everything I can to help achieve those goals.

I AGREE to cooperate in working out a realistic family budget. I will do my best to accept full responsibility for living within that budget.

I AGREE not to expect miracles in the improvement of our marriage. There is a great deal you need to know about me and I about you before we can consider ourselves truly married. But I will make every effort toward mutual knowledge and understanding.

I AGREE, on the assumption that example is the most persuasive form of argument known to man, that I will diligently seek to improve myself so I can grow into a continually better model of a marriage mate.

HIM _____

Date _____   HER _____

115

Epilogue: The Family in a Modern World

On June 18, 1940, Winston Churchill stood to address the House of Commons.

A desperate moment in British history this. British armies had been flung back on the continent, vast quantities of arms and ammunition had been lost, enemy bombers were overhead pummeling historic British cities to rubble.

At this moment the British people had called upon Churchill to be their leader.

He was a man to match the hour.

As he entered the House, the members were on their feet to cheer him to an echo, and when he rose to speak, he spoke as only Churchill could.

He was in no mood to minimize the dangers which they faced. He promised them nothing but sweat, blood, toil, and tears. Then he finished a memorable utterance with these words: "Let us brace ourselves to our duties and so bear ourselves that if the British Empire and Commonwealth last for a thousand years men will still say, 'This was their finest hour.'"

This—their finest hour—the hour of their apparent defeat?

Many of us believe Britishers were never better than they were at this moment of time.

This is a parable and an analogy of family life today.

The family is in trouble.

Dr. Paul Popenoe has written on war against the family. He says it is proceeding on a number of fronts, including:

(1) Tht cult of the playboy which assumes the female is to be exploited at will by the male. It has led to an unexpected backfire that the female has come to feel she must exploit the male.

The biological mating impulse is looked upon as a means of amusement rather than a means of building adult personality and character. This leads in turn to an emphasis on such things as apartments for swinging singles rather than the more sensible effort to provide residences ideally suited to families. The idea of responsibility gives way to a selfish hedonism.

(2) The thrust of the mass media which has vastly more financial resources than the church or school. Mass media frequently pictures every male "on the make" and implies that if he doesn't take advantage of every opportunity to exploit a female he is a chump.

(3) The homosexual campaign. Having gained access to the mass media inverts have mounted a massive campaign to gain recognition and respectability for their cause. The cry for freedom of homosexual activity among "consenting adults" is made ludicrous by the tendency of inverts to turn to younger subjects and help condition a rising generation. Almost inevitably there is a downgrading of the Judeo-Christian concept of marriage between a man and a woman, the sanctity of the family.

(4) Trial marriage. The idea that you needn't make up your mind about commitment has been with us for a long time and

has had a boost in recent days. Trial marriages being entered upon in such a casual fashion are seldom an adequate prelude to good family relationships.

(5) Divorce with no provision for counseling. Divorce proceedings are entered upon without proper consideration. As the situation stands, 30 percent of all divorce petitions filed never come to trial because the couple are reconciled. In one study 25 percent of the divorces that went through left the couples in the frame of mind in which they wanted nothing more than to have their former spouses back.

(6) The Women's Liberation Movement, which has many commendable purposes but in its aggressive drive has gone to ridiculous extremes and often degenerated into an attack on marriage, childbirth, and the family, helps to alienate many women from the idea of a vocation of home and family life.

(7) Wife swapping games. Nobody knows how widespread this procedure is but the number of people involved is probably small. However, with this emphasis on variety and pure sexuality with no commitment and the terrible potential for damaging husband-wife relationships presents a threat to the idea of a stable family.

(8) Communal enterprizes where all the women are said to be married to all the men and the children belong to the group. These experiments have been frequently tried through history and have generally been short-lived. Worse than the regularly organized groups are the so-called "communes" springing up across the country that have an almost unbelievable potential for damaging their members. With these the family is undesirable and to be avoided. Ironically many of them call themselves families trying to cash in on the associations with the word while in practice trying to tear it down.

(7) Lack of education to prepare for marriage. It is much

easier to get a marriage license than a license to drive a vehicle down the street.

This concerted attack on the family is at this moment causing a deterioration of home and family life. Many prophets of gloom are predicting the downfall of the family.

Don't you believe it! The family is a remarkably resilient unit. There have been many attacks on it before and it has bounced back.

My simple premise here projected is that some of the factors that were causing the deterioration of family life may ultimately turn out to strengthen it so this might well be the family's finest hour.

The Family Is Smaller

John Wesley was one of the greatest men who walked this earth. He stands astride the eighteenth century like a giant colossus, but no one can think of Wesley without considering the family from which he came.

Susannah Wesley, John's mother, gave birth to nineteen children and so ordered her home that she was able to give her sons and daughters enough education that the boys only had to attend prep school before moving on to Oxford University.

On Sunday afternoons she gathered her large family around her and conducted a church service so they might have religious instruction.

One night she was awakened to the smell of smoke in the house and hurrying down the hall through the doors looked back and saw to her horror that the house was afire with great sheets of flame leaping up the sides of the building. Then, to her horror, she espied the white face of five-year-old John at the second-floor window. Her husband, Reverend Samuel Wesley, tried to rush back into the house but was driven back by the flames.

Reverend Samuel Wesley fell down on his knees and commended the little boy's soul to Almighty God. But more practically minded men ran to the side of the building and one climbed up on the other's shoulder and reaching out grasped the little fellow, plucked him from the window, and dropped him to the ground.

The little boy scrambled to his feet and ran towards his mother and into her waiting arms.

As she held him close to her pregnant body, she said, "John, you're my little brand plucked from the burning."

She never let him forget this experience.

Still not satisfied with her work as a mother, she devised her celebrated plan for giving her children her individual attention. She told about it in a letter which she wrote to her husband. "On Monday I talk with Molly, on Tuesday with Hetty, Wednesday with Nancy, Thursday with Jacky, Friday with Patty, Saturday with Charles, Emily and Suky together on Sunday."

Was it any wonder she produced a John and a Charles Wesley.

Of course, Susannah was skilled in the ways of large families —she herself was one of twenty-five.

On one occasion the minister who christened Susannah and her brothers and sisters was asked, "How many children in the Annesley family? He responded, "I don't know whether it's two dozen or a quarter of a hundred.

Contrast these families—nineteen children, twenty-five children—with the average family today. Some sociologists are telling us it has 2.3 children.

There are many reasons for this shrinking family. Primarily it comes from the changing nature of the family unit.

In yesteryears's family a child was an economic asset. Take

my mother's family. She was one of twelve surviving children.

One day I asked my grandfather why he had given up dairy-ing in favor of growing alfalfa.

He replied: "If you want to be a good dairy farmer you need lots of cheap labor. The best way to do that is to have a large family. I had a large family, but when they grew up I lost my labor force and so I took to growing alfalfa."

And my mother confirmed every word he said. She told the most hair raising stories—and they never lost anything in the telling—as she described the closest thing to child slavery you could ever imagine.

She told how they were pulled out of bed at 5:30 A.M. and served a hasty breakfast so they could milk the cows. Then off to school. After school they trudged three weary miles home, had some supper, and milked the cows. Then all off to bed bright and early so they could get up next morning and milk the cows.

In those days a child was an economic asset. Stop for a moment and think about those children of yours. Consider all the things they are. I'll tell you something they are not—they're not economic assets.

See that strapping boy of yours. Do you know that by the time you take him, rear him, educate him, and get him ready to hand over to the care of some other little woman it's going to cost you from ten to thirty thousand dollars!

For these and other reasons the family is getting smaller and is going to continue to shrink.

With the passing of the large family we have lost an important laboratory of experiences for children. The skill of living is the skill of relationships, and possibilities of these experiences are increased with the size of the family. Mathematicians tell us that while in a family of two there is a possibility of only one relationship, with a family of eight there are twenty-eight possible relationships. The member of a small family is thus denied these opportunities for personal interaction.

However, with the population explosion, increased cost of child rearing and education, the smaller family may ultimately be the most reliable unit.

The Family Is More Detached

The detachment and isolation of modern life is bringing about a decay of institutions and the modern family is detached in three ways.

(1) It is detached in its locale.

As America has changed from a rural to an urban society we have witnessed a strange anomaly. In the rural areas people were widely separated spatially but close together psychologically and emotionally. As they have moved into the closely populated urban areas they are close together spatially but separated emotionally and psychologically.

The modern high-rise apartment typifies our dilemma. Many of these buildings are self-contained even having their own commissaries and locked doors to keep out all intruders. Enter once by that door and you can stay in there for the rest of your life.

New York was shocked by the murder of Kitty Genovese in middle-class Kew Gardens. It was no sudden strike. The killing stretched over an agonizing thirty-five minutes. In this period of time the killer made three murderous attacks. Kitty Genovese cried for help as she staggered along the street in a vain effort to escape. A police inquiry has revealed that during this time, thirty-seven people were awakened by the victim's screams and saw what was happening; but not one of them called the police.

The reluctance to do something was later explained by an on-looker: "I didn't want to get involved."

This lack of involvement with others is one of the most depressing features of modern urban life.

A young couple get married and move into the big city. They don't know anybody. There are no pressures of community, and the marriage can easily fall apart.

(2) It is detached by ease of divorce.

Our forefathers knew marriage was for keeps, but a modern couple is not so sure. A recent cartoon showed a young couple emerging from the Justice of the Peace's office and the bride saying, "Oh, darling, our very first wedding."

Ease of divorce is a mixed blessing and often brings in its train more problems than it solves.

I once counseled a couple who said they had come for pre-marital counseling. Now they certainly looked rather old for premarital counseling. So I asked a routine question. "Have you ever been married before?"

He had and so had she.

I further inquired, "More than once?"

Then came the story. They had both been married four times previously—to each other.

Ease of divorce overlooks the commitment element. The heart of a Christian marriage is commitment, "For better for worse for richer for poorer, in sickness and in health, till death us do part."

With the idea of permanence people work harder to make a marriage go. The prospect of an easy divorce can easily lead to a casual attitude towards the relationship.

(3) It is detached from the pressures of children.

The child-bearing habits of American women are changing.

They formerly went on having children right up through middle life.

The average American woman today has her last child at about age twenty-six and becomes a grandmother at age forty-four. If her married life is divided into two segments of twenty-eight years each, she will have twenty-eight years with children and twenty-eight years without children. Sociologists refer to these last twenty-eight years as the "empty nest" period of life.

We have not accommodated ourselves well to this new period of life, and an alarming number of marriages break up after twenty years of married life.

One of the problems is that many people have forgotten where the basic marriage loyalties lie. Our basis of loyalty is not to our parents or to our children but to our spouse.

I liked the attitude of one woman. The conference had been discussing the problems of the empty nest.

She said, "Problems of the empty nest my eye. For the first twenty years of my life I did what my parents wanted me to do, for the second twenty I did what my children wanted me to do —oh boy am I going to have a ball the next twenty."

In taking a second look at the situation if a marriage survives not because of pressures of community, stigma of divorce, pressures of community, but because the couple wants to stay together it will obviously be a better marriage.

Family Roles Are Changing.

In the rural setting family roles were fairly clearly defined. All the members were engaged in a cooperative venture to earn the living.

Father had to cultivate the crops, and as he was constantly around the farm as the visible evidence of an ever present leader, mother gave herself to the task of keeping the household on the move, cooking meals, and preserving food. Even the children had their chores which were demanded rather than being optional.

Things have changed today.

Father is away the biggest proportion of the day. He is a vague figure who only periodically appears, and the children no longer have a sense of being a part of a cooperative venture.

The biggest change of all may be the mother's role. About 40 percent of American women go to work either full or part time. For better or for worse the working wife is with us.

For many women this means an experience of self-fulfilment and extra financial power, but it also brings its problems not the least of which is the division of labor.

A young couple sat in my office and when I asked them the cause of their difficulties the little woman spoke up: "He suggested that I get a job. I wasn't over enthusiastic but I agreed, then the trouble began.

"I got home from work at 5:00 P.M. and started to fix the supper. He came in at 5:45—flopped into a chair and proceeded to read the newspaper."

Then came a vicious look into her blue eyes. "If I have to help earn the living, he's going to help with the housework."

The division of labor can easily become a sensitive spot for the working wife.

As children grow they need to see before them models of masculinity and femininity. In the developmental processes they identify with one of these models.

One of our biggest problems is what one writer has called the "taboo on tenderness."

I once asked a young man, "Tell me something about your father and mother's love life."

He looked at me in astonishment: "Love life, that's a joke.

I never ever remember seeing my father kiss my mother."

Where does this boy learn about love?

He sees his models at the movies, on television, in novels, and they probably are the most distorted portrayal of love that any one could imagine.

Husbands and wives will have to work harder at portraying the roles of masculinity and femininity.

Wanted—Mature Family Members.

In the light of all this freedom for the members of a family it will be of the utmost importance that we have family members who are mature enough to handle these situations. The word "mature" simply means to grow, and family members must grow.

There are at least three characteristics of a mature person, a capacity for self-objectification, an undergirding philosophy of life, and an extended ego.

(1) A capacity for self-objectification.

Across the portals of the temple at Delphi were inscribed the words, "Know thyself," and such is the human capacity for self-deception that few of us really know ourselves.

I once went to a store to buy a new suit, and the salesman pushed me into one of those three way mirrors in which I could see myself side on—I didn't like what I saw. I like to refer to myself as "robust" and "strong," but it was a moment of truth and other words came into my mind.

If I had that much difficulty looking at my physical appearance, you can imagine how it is when I look at my naked psyche.

(2) An undergirding philosophy of life.

The undergirding philosophy I am suggesting is faith in the One who walked the dusty roads of Palestine in a bygone day.

Jesus Christ lived amongst the people, performed his first miracle at the marriage feast, and spent much of his time in home and family situations.

At the conclusion of the Sermon on the Mount Jesus said that a person who heard his sayings and obeyed them was like a man who built his house upon a rock. If we take this building concept literally we may remind ourselves that a family needs a foundation of the collective faith of its members.

(3) An extended ego.

A mature person has the capacity to think of other people and how he relates to their lives.

The greatest enemy of family life is selfishness. In this shared experience a man must learn to deny himself and take an interest in others.

Bill Sands was the son of a California judge and ran off the rails, finally finishing up as an inmate of San Quentin penitentiary under a life sentence. While there he became involved in a senseless prison riot. As a result of this, he was put in a solitary confinement cell in that part of the penitentiary known as "The Shelf."

Lying on his bare cot, heart filled with hostility and resentment, Sands heard the click of the lock and a voice, "Bill Sands."

The name jolted him. Since his imprisonment he had always been addressed by a number. He lashed back, "No one is interested in me."

"Bill, I care."

He looked up to see Clinton Duffy, the warden of the penitentiary.

I talked with Bill Sands and asked him how he felt when Clinton Duffy uttered those words. He responded, "John, with those three words Clinton Duffy gave me back my life."

Someone in your family wants his life back.
Why not give it to him?

If we have mature family members, this will be the family's
finest hour!